NEW DIRECTIONS FOR STUDENT SERVICES

Margaret J. Barr, *Northwestern University*
EDITOR-IN-CHIEF

M. Lee Upcraft, *The Pennsylvania State University*
ASSOCIATE EDITOR

Identifying and Implementing the Essential Values of the Profession

Robert B. Young
Kent State University

EDITOR

Number 61, Spring 1993

JOSSEY-BASS PUBLISHERS
San Francisco

IDENTIFYING AND IMPLEMENTING THE ESSENTIAL VALUES
OF THE PROFESSION
Robert B. Young (ed.)
New Directions for Student Services, no. 61
Margaret J. Barr, Editor-in-Chief
M. Lee Upcraft, Associate Editor

Microfilm copies of issues and articles are available in 16mm and 35mm,
as well as microfiche in 105mm, through University Microfilms Inc., 300
North Zeeb Road, Ann Arbor, Michigan 48106.

LC 85-644751   ISSN 0164-7970   ISBN 1-55542-698-0

NEW DIRECTIONS FOR STUDENT SERVICES is part of The Jossey-Bass
Higher and Adult Education Series and is published quarterly by Jossey-
Bass Inc., Publishers, 350 Sansome Street, San Francisco, California
94104-1310 (publication number USPS 449-070). Second-class postage
paid at San Francisco, California, and at additional mailing offices. POST-
MASTER: Send address changes to New Directions for Student Services,
Jossey-Bass Inc., Publishers, 350 Sansome Street, San Francisco, California
94104-1310.

SUBSCRIPTIONS for 1993 cost $45.00 for individuals and $60.00 for institutions, agencies, and libraries.

EDITORIAL CORRESPONDENCE should be sent to the Editor-in-Chief,
Margaret J. Barr, 633 Clark Street, 2-219, Evanston, Illinois 60208-1103.

Cover photograph by Wernher Krutein/PHOTOVAULT © 1990.

 The paper used in this journal is acid-free and meets the strictest
guidelines in the United States for recycled paper (50 percent
recycled waste, including 10 percent post-consumer waste).
Manufactured in the United States of America.

CONTENTS

EDITOR'S NOTES

Student affairs has always been a valuing profession. Throughout the history of the field, its practitioners have served as models for students (Fley, 1980; Barr, 1987) and its practices have developed the behaviors and attitudes of students (Evans, 1987). Sandeen (1985, p. 3) notes that "from its inception . . . the student affairs profession has had significant responsibility for the values education of college students." He relates historical documents to this "legacy of values education" of the profession. This legacy might have prompted Cowley (1961, p. 313) to note that student affairs professionals "share a common set of values" despite the diversity of their backgrounds. This volume, *Essential Values of the Profession*, explores the nature of that common set of values.

Young and Elfrink (1991) have researched the essential values of the student affairs profession, prompted by a general concern about our values and the effort of another field, professional nursing, to define its essential values. Eighty-seven percent of the respondents to their survey agreed that it was important to determine the essential values of student affairs. Ninety-seven percent of the respondents agreed that the following seven values were essential to our field today: altruism, or concern for the welfare of others; equality, or ensurance that all people have the same rights, privileges, or status; aesthetics, or qualities of objects, events, and persons that provide satisfaction; freedom, or the capacity to exercise choice; human dignity, or the inherent worth and uniqueness of an individual; justice, or the upholding of moral and legal principles; and truth, or faithfulness to fact or reality. Some of the respondents added an eighth value, community, to the list of essential values. Community was defined as mutual empowerment. This volume continues the study of the essential values of student affairs work. Unless our profession understands its essential values, it cannot fulfill its central purposes.

Definitions and Related Issues

Scholars have not created a precise definition of values (O'Callaghan, 1983), but several describe values as beliefs that guide action toward desirable ends (for example, Raths, Harmin, and Simon, 1966; Rokeach, 1973; Morrill, 1980). Rokeach (1973) categorizes two types of values, instrumental (desirable modes of conduct) and terminal (desirable end states). These are organized into systems, enduring hierarchies of values.

Raths, Harmin, and Simon (1966) popularized values clarification, a means of exploring value systems. They believed that education should emphasize values clarification instead of values transmission, or the imposition of certain values on individuals. Many have agreed that higher education should be values-neutral and that values issues should be left entirely to individuals, but few student affairs professionals have joined that chorus (Dalton, 1985). We understand that values transmission has been a historical role of education, and most of us expect to transmit values to students directly or indirectly. Some of us might use clarification for more effective values transmission. For that purpose, the two methods are more complementary than antagonistic.

Purpose and Format of This Volume

Jon C. Dalton (this volume, p. 88) writes, "The central issue for student affairs leaders . . . is not *whether* they should advocate certain essential values but *which* values should be advocated and *how* these values can be advocated in a clear and intentional manner." This volume examines the nature of eight essential values in student affairs: aesthetics, altruism, community, equality, freedom, human dignity, justice, and truth. It looks at their historical and current interpretations within the profession and the rest of the academy. The volume affirms the importance of these values and shows the reader how to implement them through personal decision making, in teaching, and through leadership in our institutions.

The first five chapters of the volume expand the discussion of the essential values of student affairs. In Chapter One, I analyze key historical documents for information about the values of the profession.

In the next two chapters, values are clustered into two paradigms that should be familiar to readers of cognitive, feminist, or Africanist psychologies: the justice and caring paradigms, which might represent the basic value systems of faculty and of student affairs professionals, respectively. Specifically, in Chapter Two, Scott T. Rickard describes the dominance of truth, justice, and freedom in academic life. He shows how faculty have interpreted these values in the past and how we, as student affairs professionals, must be involved in their reinterpretation today. In Chapter Three, Linda M. Clement considers an alternative trio of values: altruism, equality, and human dignity. Cowley (1961, p. 313) might have been referring to these values when he noted that the values shared by student affairs professionals "by and large run counter to those of impersonalistic professors." Clement explores contemporary definitions of these values and our responsibilities in regard to them.

In Chapter Four, Dennis C. Roberts elaborates on our understanding of community, one of the earliest values of student affairs. He also looks at the ways in which community concepts can be translated into programs, services, processes, and relationships.

In Chapter Five, I describe the value of aesthetics. My focus is on how aesthetics relate to student development, assessment, cultural diversity, and administrative effectiveness.

The remaining three chapters deal with the use of values on campus. They are approached from three perspectives: decision making, education, and the organization. In Chapter Six, Victoria L. Elfrink and LuAnn Linson Coldwell discuss the role of the student affairs professional as a values practitioner. They present the INVOLVE model of decision making in student affairs practice.

In Chapter Seven, Leila V. Moore and Deborah H. Hamilton resurrect the issue of values transmission versus values clarification. They explore the formal and informal ways in which the essential values of our field can be taught to undergraduate students and to graduate students in student affairs preparation programs.

Finally, in Chapter Eight, Jon C. Dalton describes the need to implement the essential values. He examines how five different forms of values approaches affect policy, programming, and staff development within our institutions.

Robert B. Young
Editor

References

Barr, M. J. "Individual and Institutional Integrity." *NASPA Journal*, 1987, *24*, 2–6.

Cowley, W. H. *An Overview of American Colleges and Universities.* Unpublished manuscript, Department of History, Stanford University, 1961.

Dalton, J. C. "Values Education: A New Priority for College Student Development." In J. C. Dalton (ed.), *Promoting Values Development in College Students.* Monograph Series No. 4. Washington, D.C.: National Association of Student Personnel Administrators, 1985.

Evans, N. "A Framework for Assisting Student Affairs Staff in Fostering Moral Development." *Journal of Counseling and Development*, 1987, *66*, 191–194.

Fley, J. "Student Personnel Pioneers: Those Who Developed Our Profession." *NASPA Journal*, 1980, *17*, 25–44.

Morrill, R. *Teaching Values in College.* San Francisco: Jossey-Bass, 1980.

O'Callaghan, P. "Teaching Values for Adults: Graduate Programs in Liberal Studies." In M. Collins (ed.), *Teaching Values and Ethics in College.* New Directions for Teaching and Learning, no. 13. San Francisco: Jossey-Bass, 1983.

Raths, L., Harmin, M., and Simon, S. *Values and Teaching: Working with Values in the Classroom.* Columbus, Ohio: Merrill, 1966.

Rokeach, M. *The Nature of Human Values.* New York: Free Press, 1973.

Sandeen, A. "The Legacy of Values Education in College Student Personnel Work." In J. C. Dalton (ed.), *Promoting Values Development in College Students.* Monograph Series No. 4. Washington, D.C.: National Association of Student Personnel Administrators, 1985.

Young, R. B., and Elfrink, V. L. "Essential Values of Student Affairs Work." *Journal of College Student Development*, 1991, *32* (1), 47–55.

ROBERT B. YOUNG is associate professor and leader of the graduate program in higher education and student personnel at Kent State University, Kent, Ohio.

A qualitative analysis of historical documents uncovered three "domains" of essential values in student affairs: individual human dignity (with freedom, altruism, and truth), equality, and community (with justice).

The Essential Values of the Profession

Robert B. Young

> Ours is the responsibility of conserving, transmitting, rectifying, and expanding the heritage of values we have received that those that come after us may receive it more solid and secure, more widely accessible and more generously shared than we have received it.
>
> —John Dewey (1934, p. 87)

John Dewey's words seem familiar. The American Council on Education's (1986a) 1937 *The Student Personnel Point of View* (*SPPOV*) opens with the following: "One of the basic purposes of higher education is the preservation, transmittal, and enrichment of culture" (p. 76). The 1949 *SPPOV* begins, "The central purpose of higher education is the preservation, transmittal, and enrichment of culture" (American Council on Education, 1986b, p. 122). Both documents seem to borrow from Dewey, who made values synonymous with culture. Our values mission is implicit in the opening words of our two most important documents. Thus, a discussion of the essential values of our profession keeps faith with our heritage and that mission.

Values in Student Affairs

Sandeen (1985) explored several historical documents in writing about the values education legacy of student affairs. I used his technique to analyze the historical importance of eight values of the field: aesthetics, altruism, community, equality, freedom, human dignity, justice, and truth. Five documents were analyzed: Clothier's ([1931] 1986) "College Personnel Principles and Functions," Cowley's ([1936] 1986) "The Nature of Student

Personnel Work," the American Council on Education's (1986a, 1986b) 1937 and 1949 *SPPOV*, and the Council of Student Personnel Associations' (COSPA, [1972] 1986) "Student Development Services in Post-Secondary Education." The list of works was not all-inclusive, nor was the search unbiased. The eight essential values in Young and Elfrink's (1991) study were sought in the five documents in order to determine their historical nature and priority. Conclusions were organized using Spradley's (1979) semantic domain analysis technique and Rokeach's (1973) categorization of *terminal* and *instrumental* values. Rokeach defined terminal values as desirable end states and instrumental values as desirable modes of conduct to achieve those end states.

My review uncovered three domains of essential student affairs values, two of which encompassed subordinate instrumental values: human dignity (with freedom, altruism, and truth), equality, and community (with justice). Aesthetics was not mentioned enough to be included with the others. The values of human dignity and community were ordered along a continuum from the individual to the broader society, respectively, with equality reflecting aspects of both.

Human Dignity

Young and Elfrink (1991) defined human dignity as the inherent worth and uniqueness of an individual. While the label is contemporary, the definition fits one of the most important historical values of the student affairs profession.

Clothier ([1931] 1986) defined student affairs work as a systematic intervention to promote an individual's development of body, mind, and character. He emphasized the individual because the principle of individual differences was a fundamental tenet of student affairs work. Five years later, Cowley ([1936] 1986) used this definition and four others to illustrate the emphasis of our field on the individualization of education. Although Cowley thought that these definitions were too "inclusive," he still defined the personnel point of view as a "philosophy of education which puts emphasis upon the individual" (p. 69). By 1949, the emphasis was shifting to the individual in social situations. The 1949 *SPPOV* begins with a list of three new social goals for higher education. However, it notes that these goals still "affect positively the education and development of each individual student" (American Council on Education, 1986b, p. 122).

Freedom: The Instrument of Individualism. The 1949 *SPPOV* declared that the student is a responsible participant in his or her own development and not a passive recipient of knowledge and skills. The document linked individual development with responsibility; freedom must be disciplined for the fulfillment of human dignity. This point was driven home in the COSPA ([1972] 1986, p. 392) statement, which declared as its primary assumption that "human beings express their life goal as becoming free, liberated, [and] self-directed." COSPA defined student development as the process by which individuals gain increasing mastery of their own self-direction and fulfillment, thus seeming to consider freedom an end and a means, a product and process of student development.

COSPA indicated that the movement of students toward self-direction should be facilitated by student affairs professionals whose own freedom was enhanced in their graduate preparation programs. COSPA seems to imply that the personal experience of freedom is necessary for student affairs professionals to model this value for students, another indication of the instrumental nature of this value.

Altruism to Free Human Dignity. The relationship between the student affairs professional and students is described in all of the major documents of the field, but it is delineated best by Clothier ([1931] 1986). He stated that the worth of a student affairs professional was determined by his or her sincere and intelligent interest in the individual student. He linked this interest to truth and freedom when he wrote that the student affairs professional had to know each student fully in order to help him or her, and that each student was free to reject the counsel of the professional. The relationship was altruistic, not dictatorial. This was reaffirmed in the 1949 *SPPOV*, which declared that skilled student affairs professionals (specifically, counselors) must stimulate self-understanding without directing decisions.

The 1949 *SPPOV* related altruism to social service as well as to the relationship between professional staff and students. Altruism thus became a goal of education: Students should learn how to contribute to the improvement of society. Still, this goal seems connected to the student affairs value of human dignity. Colleges were supposed to fulfill their "broad responsibilities for aiding in the optimum development of the *individual* (emphasis added) in his relations to society" (American Council on Education, 1986b, p. 126).

Truth: The Instrument of Freedom and Human Dignity. Student affairs exists, in part, to define "truth" more broadly than do academicians. We have connected "faithfulness to fact" with the self-realization of students, not just their intellectual development. The COSPA statement declared that knowledge of self and environment constitutes not just ideas but the basis of teaching. Earlier, the 1949 *SPPOV* stated that teaching must include social, moral, and physical concerns as well as intellectual ones.

Each student needs full information in order to develop fully, both outside and inside the classroom. Student affairs has provided some of that information through vocational and instructional research. In 1931, Clothier stated that colleges should make full information available to students about different vocations and help students evaluate their aptitudes and interests in light of that information. The placement function of student affairs was related to a broadly conceived value of truth that was implemented through an altruistic relationship.

The importance of instructional research is apparent in these historical documents. As Clothier ([1931] 1986, p. 14) stated, "The college must recognize that research is an integral part of its [student affairs] work." Cowley ([1936] 1986, p. 56) noted that this function was primary after World War I and many still believed that the field was "nothing more than personnel research." Personnel research included instructional research because nobody else was doing it. The 1937 *SPPOV* recommended cooperation between student affairs professionals and instructors on the premise that instructors needed full information to individualize the education of students. Our efforts at research provided fuller truths to serve human dignity in the classroom.

Evolution of Equality

The emphasis of equality has shifted from individuals to groups. "Having the same rights, privileges, or status" was applied first to holistic education. Later, it included underrepresented groups in higher education.

Equal Abilities. The notion of individual dignity is closely connected with a holistic view of truth, declared as an appreciation of individual differences beyond the intellectual. Cowley's ([1936] 1986, p. 69) summary definition of our field put emphasis "upon the individual student and his all-round development as a person rather than upon his intellectual training alone."

The 1937 *SPPOV* mentioned not only the intellectual capacity of students but also their emotions, physical conditions, social relationships, vocational skills, moral and religious values, economic resources, and aesthetic appreciations. The 1949 *SPPOV* was more succinct, limiting the discussion to physical, social, emotional, intellectual, and spiritual characteristics. Regardless of the exact characteristics, the student was to be considered a whole, with equal attention paid to all attributes. As Clothier ([1931] 1986, p. 15) stated, "We are interested in the individual student's development, not in any one phase of his program such as scholarship, intellect, leadership, but from the aspect of his whole personality. We are concerned with all those methods and the procedures which bring influences to bear upon him 'of whatever nature.' "

The historical documents mandate action on behalf of equality. Clothier believed that every agency within the college had to know the diversity of student characteristics and use that knowledge to improve student success during and after college. Cowley ([1936] 1986) viewed such admonitions as the "torch" of progressive education that our profession carried to faculty who considered only the student's mind. Thus, Cowley retraced our path of values to Dewey.

Equal People. President Truman's Commission on Higher Education emphasized the importance of good citizenship as a goal of education (President's Commission on Higher Education, 1948). It recommended the expansion of higher education opportunities for more citizens, eventually assisting the community college movement in the United States. The 1949 *SPPOV* reflected the goals of that report, thus our value of equality began to include different social groups. That *SPPOV* makes indirect allusions to disadvantaged groups in society, whom socially conscious students were supposed to help. The only direct expressions concern the staffing of student affairs offices. The 1949 *SPPOV* stated that competent male and female counselors should be available to students who preferred to consult with a man or a woman.

Most of these historical documents antedate recent social movements. For example, contemporary authors (for example, Hammond, 1981; Sandeen, 1985) have discussed the impact of civil rights on the student affairs profession. The COSPA ([1972] 1986, p. 392) statement indicated that professionals bear responsibility toward the "broad spectrum of persons who can profit from post-secondary education," presumably without bias, because "the potential for development and self-direction is possessed by everyone" (p. 393). The COSPA statement contains another interesting and more specific declaration about equal people. One of its keystones is that "students are viewed as collaborators with the faculty and administration" (p. 391), putting to rest *in loco parentis* during the last years of student activism.

Community and One of Its Instruments, Justice

Roberts (this volume) notes that community has always been a value of the student affairs profession. The 1949 *SPPOV* stated that "the development of students as whole persons interacting in social situations is the central concern" (American Council on Education, 1986b, p. 122) of student affairs, but the document focused more on individual than on social relationships.

Cowley ([1936] 1986) contrasted relationships between students and business officers, faculty, and student affairs professionals. Business relationships were essentially impersonal, instructional relationships focused on instruction, and student affairs relationships consisted of all other activities related to personal development. Thus, personal *empowerment* (half of the definition in Young and Elfrink, 1991) was a distinctive purpose of student affairs relationships in the campus community.

Both the 1937 and the 1949 *SPPOV* focused on campus community with limited additional references to broader communities. They listed functions related to the development of campus community and described the need for collaboration among student affairs officers and others to create campus community.

The 1949 *SPPOV* listed eleven student needs that require "opportunities for intensive classroom learning supplemented by many of the major elements of community living. Students live, work, make friends, have fun, make financial ends meet—all within the community of scholars" (American Council on Education, 1986b, p. 126). One need is orientation to the college environment, so that students "feel at home" (p. 127). Admissions and orientation functions are listed under this need, the same student affairs functions that received first mention in the 1937 *SPPOV*. Another need in the 1949 *SPPOV* is "a sense of belonging to the college" (p. 128). Students must find a role in relation to others that will make them feel valued, contribute to their feelings of self-worth, and contribute to a feeling of kinship with others—in other words, they need to be empowered through community.

The 1937 *SPPOV* extended the value of community beyond the campus. Student affairs had to help college graduates understand the "social, recreational, and cultural interests of the community. Such concern implies their willingness to assume those individual and social responsibilities which are essential to the common good" (American Council on Education, 1986a, p. 83). As noted earlier, the 1949 *SPPOV* reflected the goals of the Truman Commission on Higher Education to improve citizenship education after World War II. Good citizenship was an obligation of all graduates.

The 1937 *SPPOV* urged cooperation among student affairs officers on individual campuses and nationally. This might reflect Cowley's ([1936] 1986) influence on that document. He closed his essay with an opinion that personnel officers should be working together at local and national levels. He added that such cooperation required an appreciation of the unity of the diverse functions of our field. The 1937 *SPPOV* advocated national cooperation and leadership, noting the development of professional associations for student affairs administrators and counselors. This extension of our professional community across campuses was evident in Young and Elfrink's (1991) findings about community.

Cowley's document distinguished between the student personnel point of view and student personnel work. The personnel point of view reminded everyone on campus, especially faculty, of the need to mutually empower students. Each of the historical documents contains advice for faculty. While our field reacted against their focus on intellectual truth, it also sought their cooperation in holistic individual development. Specifically, Cowley related our efforts in instructional research to the empowerment of faculty. Few faculty were prepared to research student characteristics, even though it would have increased their effectiveness as teachers. The 1937 *SPPOV* made the same comment, perhaps because of Cowley's participation in that project.

As noted earlier, COSPA ([1972] 1986, p. 391) declared that students were "collaborators" with faculty and administrators in the process of learning. This reflected the value of equality and it took the value of community as mutual empowerment to a new level. The 1949 *SPPOV* stated only that students could make "significant contributions" (American Council on Education, 1986b, p. 138) to the development of effective student affairs programs.

Current wisdom links justice with individualist values such as freedom and truth (for example, Kohlberg, 1969; Rickard, this volume). Although justice (through discipline) is connected to individual human dignity in the historical documents of student affairs, it seems more properly connected to the value of community. This is its apparent priority; it is not disconnected from either the individual or the group. The 1937 *SPPOV* stated that the goals of discipline are that "the individual will be strengthened, and the welfare of the group preserved" (American Council on Education, 1986a, p. 78).

Rhatigan (1978) wrote that there was almost no chapter on discipline in *Pieces of Eight* (Appleton, Briggs, and Rhatigan, 1978), a book about chief student affairs officers. He argued that our field did not understand the central, values education purposes of one of its original functions. The 1937 *SPPOV* affirmed the fact that the first student affairs officers were appointed to relieve administrators and faculties of discipline problems. However, this statement did not address the goal of discipline, the value(s) that it might serve. The historical documents in this review made few references to those purposes of discipline.

While discipline is a justice function, the 1949 *SPPOV* related it to student development as well. The value of upholding moral and legal principles is connected to "an educational function, designed to modify personal behavior patterns and to substitute socially acceptable attitudes for those which have precipitated unacceptable behavior" (American Council on Education, 1986b, p. 133). Discipline was considered a special case of counseling for the development of responsible behavior, not simply punishment for misbehavior. This seemed to fit the values conception of empowerment within the campus community. It also elevated our discipline activities above legal interests, to the moral plane.

The historical documents related the value of justice to activities other than discipline. For example, Clothier ([1931] 1986) noted that the college should not select students with negligible chances for success. The 1949 *SPPOV* said that students deserved teaching and courses that fit their characteristics and the purposes of the curriculum. These suggestions related fairness to the actions of the campus community. Students needed just treatment in order to be empowered by the college.

Case for Aesthetics

Few student affairs professionals today would include aesthetics in a list of their essential values (Young and Elfrink, 1991), and few references were made to aesthetics in the documents reviewed here. Aesthetic appreciations were listed with the other holistic interests of students in the 1937 *SPPOV*. That document also described a need for "creative imagination" (American Council on Education, 1986a, p. 76), potentially an aesthetic concern. Aesthetics received indirect recognition in two of the eleven areas of student needs that were listed in the 1949 *SPPOV*: the understanding and use of emotions, and the development of lively and significant interests. In sum, however, aesthetics did not seem to be an essential value in the historical documents reviewed. It is an important value, but considerable discussion needs to occur before aesthetics can be accepted as an essential value of student affairs (see Young, this volume, Chapter Five; Young and Elfrink, 1991).

Evolving Nature of Values

This review of historical documents revealed the primacy of three values in student affairs: human dignity, which involved the instrumental values of freedom, altruism, and truth; equality; and community, which involved the instrumental value of justice. Individual human dignity seemed to be the most essential historical value, given the commentary about it and the support from other values. Equality underwent a transition from the individual to the group. Community focused on students in the campus setting, but it contained hints of a nascent professional community of student affairs administrators.

Our values seem somewhat different today. Factors such as cultural diversity have affected them. This evolution is only natural because internal and external factors always change values priorities (Morrill, 1980). Such changes mandate further review of the essential values of student affairs. Which are eternal and which are ephemeral? How can we use our values well? The other chapters in this volume seek answers to these questions.

References

American Council on Education. "The Student Personnel Point of View." In G. Saddlemire and A. Rentz (eds.), *Student Affairs: A Profession's Heritage*. Media Publication No. 40. Alexandria, Va.: American College Personnel Association, 1986a. (Originally published 1937.)

American Council on Education. "The Student Personnel Point of View." In G. Saddlemire and A. Rentz (eds.), *Student Affairs: A Profession's Heritage*. Media Publication No. 40. Alexandria, Va.: American Council Personnel Association, 1986b. (Originally published 1949.)

Appleton, J., Briggs, C., and Rhatigan, J. (eds.). *Pieces of Eight*. Portland, Oreg.: National Institute for Research and Development, 1978.

Clothier, R. C. "College Personnel Principles and Functions." In G. Saddlemire and A. Rentz (eds.), *Student Affairs: A Profession's Heritage*. Media Publication No. 40. Alexandria, Va.: American College Personnel Association, 1986. (Originally published 1931.)

Council of Student Personnel Associations. "Student Development Services in Post-Secondary Education." In G. Saddlemire and A. Rentz (eds.), *Student Affairs: A Profession's Heritage*. Media Publication No. 40. Alexandria, Va.: American College Personnel Association, 1986. (Originally published 1972.)

Cowley, W. H. "The Nature of Student Personnel Work." In G. Saddlemire and A. Rentz (eds.), *Student Affairs: A Profession's Heritage*. Media Publication No. 40. Alexandria, Va.: American College Personnel Association, 1986. (Originally published 1936.)

Dewey, J. *A Common Faith*. New Haven, Conn.: Yale University Press, 1934.

Hammond, E. "The New Student-Institutional Relationship: Its Impact on Student Affairs Administration." *NASPA Journal*, 1981, *19* (2), 17–21.

Kohlberg, L. "Continuities and Discontinuities in Childhood and Adult Moral Development." *Human Development*, 1969, *12*, 93–120.

Morrill, R. *Teaching Values in College*. San Francisco: Jossey-Bass, 1980.

President's Commission on Higher Education. *Higher Education for American Democracy: The Report of the President's Commission on Higher Education*. New York: HarperCollins, 1948.

Rhatigan, J. "There Was Almost No Chapter on Discipline." In J. Appleton, C. Briggs, and J. Rhatigan (eds.), *Pieces of Eight*. Portland, Oreg.: National Institute for Research and Development, 1978.

Rokeach, M. *The Nature of Human Values*. New York: Free Press, 1973.

Sandeen, A. "The Legacy of Values Education in College Student Personnel Work." In J. C. Dalton (ed.), *Promoting Values Development in College Students*. Monograph Series No. 4. Washington, D.C.: National Association of Student Personnel Administrators, 1985.

Spradley, J. P. *The Ethnographic Interview*. Troy, Mo.: Holt, Rinehart & Winston, 1979.

Young, R. B., and Elfrink, V. L. "Essential Values of Student Affairs Work." *Journal of College Student Development*, 1991, *32* (1), 47–55.

ROBERT B. YOUNG *is associate professor and leader of the graduate program in higher education and student personnel at Kent State University, Kent, Ohio.*

Although truth, freedom, and justice are the traditional values of the academy, their definitions and applications are changing and student affairs professionals should be involved in these changes.

Truth, Freedom, Justice: Academic Tradition and the Essential Values

Scott T. Rickard

An assemblage of issues has fragmented higher education and challenged the established meaning of its core values of truth, freedom, and justice. Common agreement on these values is in question because of the conflicts between historically accepted views and more contemporary interpretations. The code words for these contemporary issues include multiculturalism, tolerance, diversity, free speech, censorship, racism, sexism, civility, and political correctness. Whatever the terms in use, it is obvious that there are conflicts in higher education about the definition and the application of truth, freedom, and justice.

The conflicts occur because various individuals and groups hold different interpretations of truth, freedom, and justice. As participants, facilitators, and sometimes instigators of the clash of values, student affairs professionals need to understand the historical background of the core academic values, assess the implications of contemporary points of view, and actively engage in shaping the future meanings of these values.

Truth

For generations, higher education has defined its primary role as the protection and dissemination of truth. This definition naturally leads to key questions: What is the nature of truth? How is truth determined? And how do traditional notions of truth converge and conflict with contemporary notions of truth? These questions have engaged philosophers from the time of ancient Greece to the present.

In their study of the professoriate, Bowen and Schuster (1986) identified the primary functions of higher education as the pursuit and dissemination of learning. They referred to learning in this context as "the truth—that which, so far as possible, is judged to be true" (p. 53). Bowen and Schuster observed that faculty members are expected to preserve and promulgate "the truth" even when its pursuit is unpopular.

Over the history of higher education, the curriculum has been the primary vehicle for the dissemination of knowledge, which represents truth. It is thus understandable why faculty place such importance on the definition of general education requirements, the sequencing of courses, and course requirements for graduation.

In recent years, the debate about the curriculum (and hence truth) has taken on an intense and somewhat different tone. From the trivium and quadrivium of classical antiquity to the smorgasbord of courses offered in most colleges and universities today, the curriculum has implicitly reflected prevailing views about truth. Because of increased diversity within higher education, new viewpoints are challenging the traditional notions of what constitutes truth and how it is determined. The curriculum has become a battleground for conflicting views of truth represented by traditionalists and multiculturalists. To illustrate, Rothenberg (1991) describes the paradigm shift from an objective, Eurocentric curriculum to a subjective, multicultural one. She contends that the traditional curriculum represents the interests and perspectives of privileged, white, European males. It is viewed as neutral and objective and the standard against which everything else is measured. She notes that the books in this curriculum are referred to as literature and honored as timeless and universal, while the books of others are labeled as transitory and idiosyncratic. Rothenberg advocates a curriculum of greater inclusion, believing that the traditional curriculum has too narrow a view of truth.

Others view the efforts to redefine the nature of the curriculum as a new form of 1960s-style radicalism, characterized by politics rather than dispassionate scholarship. Truth is determined by power (Pfaff, 1991).

The current debate over the nature of the curriculum may be too divisive and simplistic. Hooker (1991, p. 8) says that "we tend to oversimplify as 'either/or' the choice between the traditional Eurocentric curriculum and a curriculum of inclusion." He adds that "too many times the arguments against the so-called canon are arguments against a straw person. The canon doesn't exist; there isn't one. And even if there were one, it isn't taught on our campuses. We don't have agreement on what our students should learn" (p. 8).

As educators within the academy, student affairs professionals need to understand the nature of this debate about truth and the curriculum because it is so central to the future of our institutions. Student affairs professionals bring to this debate an understanding of the student population, its demographics, and its developmental needs. These perspectives may help faculty and other institutional leaders find common ground in this debate and thus maintain a curriculum that helps students and faculty connect in significant ways.

The curriculum debate is important to student affairs professionals from another perspective. Constructive critics of higher education have noted that our delivery of education is fragmented (Boyer, 1987). Student affairs professionals who understand the curriculum aims of their institutions can shape the extracurricular—or cocurricular—program to complement and support the academic enterprise.

Another perspective on issues of truth relates to the "curriculum" of student affairs. An emergent perspective views this curriculum as values education (for example, Welty, 1989). Some educators have noted that we need to infuse into our education outcomes a concern for community values and the development of citizenship (Boyer, 1987). Student affairs practitioners need to develop clear goals, coherent programs, and outcomes that are assessable in this realm.

As noted earlier, for generations higher education has described its role as the definer and disseminator of truth. Student affairs practitioners need to engage in this debate and participate in the definition of truth.

Freedom

The concept of academic freedom originated in the universities of medieval Europe (Wieruszowski, 1966). In the German universities of the nineteenth century, academic freedom included two meanings: "lehrfreiheit—the right of the university professor to freedom of inquiry and to freedom of teaching, the right to study and to report on his findings in an atmosphere of consent and lernfreiheit—the absence of administrative coercion" (Rudolph, 1962, p. 412) or control over students regarding such matters as what students study and where they live. With the demise of in loco parentis, student freedom from external controls has increased, and the politically correct movement has raised questions about diminished freedom of inquiry for faculty.

Bowen and Schuster (1986, p. 53) define academic freedom today as "the right of faculty members to substantial autonomy in the conduct of their work, and to freedom of thought and expression as they discover and disseminate learning. This freedom is essential to the advancement of learning." In this definition, they link the essential values of truth and freedom. In recognizing the interdependent nature of the truth and freedom, Ylvisaker (1990) asked, "Freedom for what?" He says that the traditional answer—"the search for truth demands and justifies freedom—may not be sufficient to respect academic freedom from encroachments on autonomy" (p. 15).

Academic freedom has been challenged over the past several decades. Specifically, challenges to academic freedom have been influenced by science, Darwinism, big business, war, the American Association of University Professors, and loyalty oaths (Metzger, 1985). Slaughter (1988) reviewed the rapidly changing environments of academic freedom and identified several new challenges to it. From her perspective, these contemporary challenges to academic freedom included "retrenchment and the crisis in state funding, the emerging agenda for national reform and accountability, the politicization of expertise, and the rise of new research funding patterns that emphasize government-university-industrial partnerships, especially in defense" (p. 241). Slaughter recognized that as more authorities external to higher education exert control over it, faculty lose their independence and their abilities to direct their agendas.

Current threats to academic freedom have been compared to the McCarthy era, for example, the *Newsweek* headline "Taking Offense: Is This the New Enlightenment or the New McCarthyism?" (Moline, 1991). Donald Kagan, dean of the college at Yale University, underscored the view of reduced freedom of faculty. He noted, "There is an imposed conformity of opinion. It takes real courage to oppose the orthodoxies. To tell you the truth, I was a student during the days of Joseph McCarthy, and there is less freedom now than there was then" (D'Souza, 1991, p. B1).

Trow (1985) noted that the value of academic freedom in the university is perennially at risk because of the centrality of academic freedom to teaching and learning. The very nature of freedom of inquiry threatens the status quo—the prevailing orthodoxies of various external groups such as the state and religious or political groups. Trow expressed additional concern about threats to academic freedom from inside the academy; students and others may threaten or intimidate teachers and researchers who hold unpopular views or otherwise interfere with free inquiry and the discussion of contentious issues. Trow's comments bring to mind the debate about political correctness and its impact on basic academic freedom (Moline, 1991).

Trow's commentary was precipitated by the disruption of former U.N. ambassador Jeane Kirkpatrick's speech at the University of California, Berkeley. Trow maintained that the disruption of a speaker goes well beyond issues of free speech to fundamental issues of academic freedom—the freedom to teach and learn and not just to speak. Trow went on to suggest that politicization has kept many speakers from receiving a civil reception at many of the leading colleges and universities.

This concern expressed in the mid-1980s continues into the 1990s, as witnessed by the cancellation of an invited speech by Linda Chavez at the University of Northern Colorado. As reported by D'Souza (1991), Linda Chavez was invited to speak about her book, *Out of the Barrio,* on Hispanic American politics and assimilation. She was disinvited because her stand on the issue of bilingualism was very controversial among minority students. In this situation, the politics of race circumscribed truth and limited freedom of expression.

Derek Bok, former president of Harvard, made an eloquent and compelling case for the relationships between freedom of expression and academic freedom: "Freedom of expression, in all its forms, can be justified on two fundamental grounds. For the individual, the right to speak and write as one chooses is a form of liberty that contributes in important ways to a rich and stimulating life. To be deprived of such liberty is to lose the chance to participate fully in an intellectual exchange that helps to develop one's values, to make one's meaning of the world, to exercise those qualities of mind and imagination that are most distinctively human. Beyond its significance to the individual, freedom of speech has traditionally been regarded in this country as important to the welfare of society" (1982, p. 18).

Syndicated columnist Nat Hentoff (1991) described an incident at Harvard that put Bok's principles to the test. A twenty-one-year-old pre-law student, named Kerrigan, hung a Confederate flag from her fourth-floor campus residence. She did it out of regional pride and to test "Harvard's Northeast liberal establishment." She said, " 'If they talk about diversity, they're gonna get it. If they talk about tolerance, they better be ready to have it.' " Hentoff reported that "they were not ready. The pressures on Kerrigan to deep-six that flag were intense and unremitting. There were protest marches, forums, letters and editorials in the campus papers, an angry session with her fellow students living at Kirkland House, and most wounding of all, a letter delivered to each member of 'the Kirkland House Community' written by the faculty housemasters."

Hentoff reported that the issues intensified when "19-year-old Jacinda Townsend, a Harvard junior from Kentucky who is black, spray-painted a Nazi swastika on a white bedsheet and hung it in her window. It would emphasize, she said, that Kerrigan's flag is a symbol of genocide to many blacks. That's why, Townsend added, 'Kerrigan's flag is very frightening to me. I don't see it so much as part of free speech, but as a threat of violence.' "

Hentoff concluded that "Townsend figured that the swastika would be so outrageous that the university would force removal of both her message and that of Kerrigan. It didn't happen. Outgoing Harvard President Derek Bok declared the display of both symbols 'insensitive and unwise,' but he pointed out that Harvard's commitment to free speech prevents the banning of either form of expression 'simply because [they offend] the feelings of many members of the community.' "

In situations like this case at Harvard, student affairs professionals are frequently placed in untenable positions. They are expected to control student behavior for the purpose of honoring civility and minimizing adverse public relations while also honoring freedom of expression. The delicate balancing of competing institutional values requires thoughtful judgments and Solomon-like decisions in the context of politicized incidents. Although particular circumstances may occasionally allow for the affirmation of both values, this does not appear to be the usual outcome. Either freedom or civility is supported at the expense of the other, with negative consequences. To respect civility at the expense of freedom is to jeopardize an educational role with students and to be viewed by faculty as opposed to fundamental values of academic freedom; and to support academic freedom over diversity or civility is to risk charges of insensitivity, prejudice, or racism.

The courts have recently ruled on issues of civility and free speech. A University of Michigan policy was revised after a federal court rejected it in 1989. In Wisconsin, a federal judge struck down a University of Wisconsin speech code that barred slurs or epithets based on a person's race, sex, religion, sexual orientation, disability, or ethnic origin (Collison, 1991). Nine students had been disciplined for creating a hostile learning environment. More recently, the Supreme Court struck down a hate crimes law; this ruling cast serious doubt about the constitutionality of campus speech codes that punish students for offensive remarks.

Because of the traditional role of *in loco parentis*, student affairs staff have had to enforce civility at the expense of freedom of expression. The inherent danger of this role is to be perceived by faculty as agents of "politically correct" behavior. Clashes between academic freedom and the notion of civility will continue on our college campuses, and student affairs staff will be called on to educate, facilitate, and sometimes rule on such matters. We must act in this arena to uphold freedom of expression as an essential value while at the same time striving to exert strong influence on those who commit acts that threaten the rights of all to be full participants in our learning communities.

Justice

Perhaps the first great philosophical question was "What is justice?" This was the question that Socrates asked at the beginning of Plato's *Republic* and it has been asked ever since (Solomon, 1990).

Bellah and others (1985) have identified three forms of justice. *Procedural* justice concerns the fairness of the rules under which society operates and disputes are adjudicated. *Distributive* justice involves the fairness of society's system of rewards and distribution of goods and opportunities. *Substantive* justice deals with the institutional order of society as a whole and its fairness.

Procedural justice, in the form of due process, has been a fundamental value of the student affairs profession regarding the adjudication of student discipline cases (see Young, this volume, Chapter One). With respect to cases involving civility and freedom of expression, it is clear that notions of justice and freedom are at loggerheads. What is considered fair or just by a group championing diversity may be considered unjust by another group supporting freedom of expression. As Dalton (this volume) notes, the conflict of values is endemic to the nature of higher education and needs to be acknowledged as an essential feature of the enterprise. Because the academic community cannot always agree on what is truth, issues involving freedom and justice often lack clear resolution.

At the center of many campus issues are conflicting views about distributive justice. For example, some multiculturalists believe that the curriculum should be more inclusive because it is just to make it more accurately reflect the diversity of students. Others, part of the "minority victim's revolution" (Rothenberg, 1991), relate their concerns about justice to a lack of fairness in the distribution of goods and opportunities within the academy.

Whether the issue involves admissions, financial aid, or student discipline, the issue also relates to definitions of distributive justice. As the conscience of the campus, student affairs professionals have multiple challenges regarding issues of distributive justice. They need to take the lead in developing and explaining policies and procedures that may seem unjust to some members of the campus community.

Ylvisaker (1990, pp. 15–16) seems to call substantive justice, "social justice," which he defines as "fairness and equity in the distribution of opportunity, in the treatment of individuals, in the assurance of personal and economic security, and in the protection of civil human rights." He identified three ways in which higher education can promote social justice in the community: (1) by renewing its commitment to the historical mission of freedom and social justice, (2) by ensuring that the campus models the ideals and practices of a free and just society, and (3) by encouraging its members to enter both individually and institutionally into a struggle for freedom and social justice in the surrounding society.

Rawls (1971) determined that the "least among us" serves as the critical test of social justice, undergirding with philosophical principles such practices as preferential admissions for African American and Hispanic American students. However, these practices rarely get discussed on campuses, and, as a result, the basic philosophical justification for them does not become part of public discourse. Affirmative action for these groups of students can be viewed as discrimination in favor of historically disadvantaged groups and "morally justified under principles of compensatory, retributive, and distributive justice" (Hooker, 1991, p. 7).

Conclusion

As noted previously, the core values of the academy are being reinterpreted in the context of contemporary values. Their priorities and relationships seem to be competing and shifting. Sanford (1980) has identified a hierarchy of values in higher education, with truth as the highest value, in an order that also includes justice and freedom and "care." He has noted the complex interdependence among these values: "Without some minimum of caring and being cared for, justice will not become an important value; if people do not have justice, they are unlikely fully to appreciate freedom, and without freedom, they will lack both the capability and the disposition to seek the truth" (p. 202). By including values of care among the essential values of higher education, Sanford seems to have added contemporary components to the traditional debate about the values priorities of the academy. He raises concerns that are examined in Clement (this volume) about the values of equality, human dignity, and altruism.

Student affairs professionals need to understand and appreciate that the eminence of equally desirable core values has always been and will always be debated within the academy. Truth, freedom, and justice are in conflict and will likely remain so throughout the 1990s. Contemporary issues place student affairs professionals in the cross fire of these conflicts, especially when they raise concerns about the worth of people. The balancing of civility, freedom, truth, and justice requires student affairs professionals to understand the competing claims of these values to eminence in higher education *and* to help students understand the nature of these values. Only through this understanding can student affairs professionals be active participants and educators instead of bystanders and antiquated administrative control agents in American higher education.

References

Bellah, R. N., and others. *Habits of the Heart: Individualism and Commitment in American Life.* New York: HarperCollins, 1985.

Bok, D. *Beyond the Ivory Tower: Social Responsibilities of the Modern University.* Cambridge, Mass.: Harvard University Press, 1982.

Bowen, H., and Schuster, J. *American Professors: A National Resource Imperiled.* New York: Oxford University Press, 1986.

Boyer, E. L. *College: The Undergraduate Experience in America.* New York: HarperCollins, 1987.

Collison, M. "Hate-Speech Code at U. of Wisconsin Voided by Court." *Chronicle of Higher Education,* Oct. 23, 1991, pp. A1, A37.

D'Souza, D. "In the Name of Academic Freedom, Colleges Should Back Professors Against Students' Demands for 'Correct' Views." *Chronicle of Higher Education,* Apr. 24, 1991, pp. B1–B3.

Hentoff, N. "Stars and Bars at Harvard." *Washington Post,* July 13, 1991, p. A19.

Hooker, M. "Facing Our Challenges." *AAHE Bulletin,* 1991, *43* (9), 7–8.

Metzger, W. *Academic Freedom in the Age of the University.* New York: Columbia University Press, 1985.

Moline, J. "Academic Freedom and Its Responsibilities: I. What Is Academic Freedom?" Paper presented at the annual meeting of the American Conference of Academic Deans, Saint Louis, January 1991.

Pfaff, W. "A New Style of Radical Stalks Academic Freedom." *Washington Post,* June 6, 1991, p. A22.

Rawls, J. *A Theory of Justice.* Cambridge, Mass.: Harvard University Press, 1971.

Rothenberg, P. "Critics of Attempts to Democratize the Curriculum Are Waging a Campaign to Misrepresent the Work of Responsible Professors." *Chronicle of Higher Education,* Apr. 10, 1991, pp. B1, B3.

Rudolph, F. *The American College and University: A History.* New York: Knopf, 1962.

Sanford, N. *Learning After College.* Orinda, Calif.: Montaigne, 1980.

Slaughter, S. "Academic Freedom and the State." *Journal of Higher Education,* 1988, *59* (3), 241–262.

Solomon, R. *A Passion for Justice.* Reading, Mass.: Addison-Wesley, 1990.

Trow, M. "The Threat from Within: Academic Freedom and Negative Evidence." *Change,* 1985, *17* (4), 8–9, 61–64.

Welty, J. "Values Education as an Opportunity for Collaboration: A President's Perspective." *NASPA Journal,* 1989, *26,* 21–26.

Wieruszowski, H. *The Medieval University.* New York: Van Nostrand Reinhold, 1966.

Ylvisaker, P. "Promoting Social Justice: From the Campus to the Community." *Educational Record,* 1990, *71* (4), 15–18.

SCOTT T. RICKARD *is executive director of the Association of College Unions-International, Bloomington, Indiana.*

In a community in which an ethic of care is operationalized, the values of equality, altruism, and human dignity assume their appropriate importance. These values modify and enrich the traditional values of higher education.

Equality, Human Dignity, and Altruism: The Caring Concerns

Linda M. Clement

> Caring is the virtue that is born from the struggle to take responsibility.
>
> —Don Browning (1973, p. 63)

Browning's definition of care is an appropriate umbrella for the values of equality, human dignity, and altruism. All three of these values represent media for the expression of care. Kolb (1984) acknowledges that care, or, as he defines it, the drive to preserve the species, is an important human imperative. A challenge for all humans, and for college students in particular, is to define one's self in relation to others and to find meaningful ways to express care.

Today's college campuses abound with challenges, dilemmas, and opportunities related to equality, human dignity, and altruism. Issues related to these values are complex; they involve confrontations of intellect and emotion. As practitioners encounter issues related to caring values, we need to honor the importance of these issues and recognize their special relationships to the values expressed in *The Student Personnel Point of View* (American Council on Education, 1937, 1949): the holistic view of students, the recognition of individual differences, and the affirmation of community.

Equality

During the last few decades, there have been unprecedented demands for equal treatment by different groups within our society. While notions of equality have traditionally been associated with race and the civil rights movement, the agenda of equality has become the leading issue for other liberation movements, such as those of women; gay, lesbian, and bisexual students; and physically and learning-challenged students. While the goals and strategies of each of these liberation movements have some commonalities, the movements have essentially remained distinct, with agendas that are sometimes perceived as competing (Giddings, 1984). The pressures of these movements, in concert with federal legislation, judicial intervention, and leadership in higher education, have resulted in institutional changes in programs, policies, services, and curricula. Some observers say that the changes have not been enough and that true equality still eludes us (Fleming, 1984; Green, 1989). Others say that the changes have eroded the core of our institutions and have fragmented our sense of purpose and community (Bloom, 1987; D'Souza, 1991).

In the coming decade, increased turmoil and debate about issues of equality are likely as financial resources grow scarce. Even the most optimistic scenario for higher education in the near future predicts declining college enrollments (Levine and Associates, 1989). Bleak economic forecasts predict increasing tuition costs and declining public and private financial support for higher education. In this era of "doing more with less," issues of access, opportunity, and priorities will focus attention on the core value of equality (McPherson, 1983). Already we see institutions limiting access to those who cannot afford to finance themselves (Jordan, 1992), and we see institutions reducing or eliminating academic program offerings and student services (Hauptman, 1991). Hence, it is imperative that student affairs practitioners understand how the value of equality is evidenced in the higher education environment and how the choices of institutions and individuals can support or detract from commitments to equality.

Equality as a Continuum of Choice. Most responsible members of the higher education community would support a commitment to equality as a moral imperative and as a social good. Beyond this basic commitment, the debate about equality lies in its definition, and in the different programs, policies, and actions that emanate from that definition.

Consider the definition of equality as falling somewhere along a continuum. At one extreme of this continuum, equality is viewed as "equality of opportunity." Under this definition of equality, opportunities for people with the same abilities and aspirations should not be affected by their social class. Expressed in its simplest mode, where people wind up should be independent of where they start out (Rawls, 1971). An example of a policy associated with this perspective is need-blind admissions, in which student admissions to colleges or universities are based solely on their academic ability with no consideration of the students' ability to finance their educations. Another example is the requirement of nondiscrimination clauses in the charters of student groups. A third example is the random assignment of roommates, with no consideration given to race, religion, ethnic background, or geographical origin. Policies and procedures such as these represent "equal opportunity," have great face validity, and would likely receive widespread support in the higher education community.

On the other end of the continuum, equality is defined as "fair opportunity," which encompasses equal opportunity but, in addition, calls for interventions to offset the effects of inequities of socioeconomic backgrounds, family circumstances, and historical discrimination (Rawls, 1971). Rooted in this perspective is the assumption that equal opportunity alone will not ensure justice (Bellah and others, 1985). Examples of programs and services associated with this perspective are collaborative efforts with inner-city middle and high schools, differentiation in financial aid and scholarships for underrepresented populations, cultural houses and residence halls, special support services for students with disabilities, and specialized curricula such as women's studies and African American studies. These types of programs reflect the notion that equality necessitates fair opportunity and that this is only possible when there is "redress," which requires disproportionate attention to those born into inequitable positions in society (Rawls, 1971). Fair-opportunity devices have been praised by some as great equalizers, with education viewed as the appropriate vehicle. They have also been criticized by others as failing to ameliorate inequities, and, in fact, as perpetuating them (Okun, 1975).

Through their policies and programs, institutions of higher education have placed themselves in positions somewhere along the continuum between equal opportunity and fair opportunity. As institutions respond to tightening economic times and increasingly conservative political pressures, they will grapple with where they define their positions on this continuum. As institutions struggle with this issue, it is important that they emerge with clarity about their commitments to equality and to the implications for equality of their programs, policies, and services.

Challenges for Student Affairs. Challenges for practitioners in student affairs involve resolution of their own ambiguities about equality, clarification of any confusion between equality and diversity, and identification of ways that members of campus communities can realize true commitments to equality. Practitioners do not have a uniform view of equality. In Young and Elfrink's (1991) work in defining the essential values, equality was the only value revised in a major way by study participants. Some deleted the term or placed it as a subset of another term; others expanded the notion using new terminology, for example, multiculturalism, and added new terms that implied commitments well beyond equal opportunity. The views of participants in this study reflected the struggle to sort out feelings and terminology regarding equal opportunity and fair opportunity.

This struggle is probably related, in some measure, to confusion of the terms equality and diversity. As federal desegregation mandates and broad societal commitments have been embraced, equality and diversity have been used interchangeably. For example, as institutions have strived to meet court-ordered desegregation goals, often defined by numbers or percentages, fair-opportunity initiatives have been applied to all people of particular racial categories. This practice has negative implications since institutions focus more on the accomplishment of a number count and less on the true diversity of people in particular racial subgroups, sometimes resulting in failures to retain and graduate students of color. Greater attention needs to be given to individual differences among students, to the design of services to support students from all backgrounds and at all levels, and to the progression and graduation rates of students from all groups struggling for equality.

In concert with the above efforts, student affairs practitioners will need to help their campus communities establish environments that reflect a commitment to equality. This task will entail the design and implementation of programs that help members of the community establish their own understandings of equality. It also will involve the adaptation of policies, procedures, and campus environments so that they are truly hospitable to diverse populations, and the development of services and programs that support but do not separate students from different backgrounds.

Human Dignity

Although seemingly the most basic of human rights, human dignity has been a value over which we have struggled for centuries. As early as the eighteenth century, during the period of the Enlightenment, Gabriel de Mebley and Jean-Jacques Rousseau were thought radical for advocating privileges for "everyman," not just the privileged classes (Burns and Ralph, 1974). Early in our history, we asserted the importance of human rights by adding the Bill of Rights to our Constitution. This country's subsequent struggles over civil rights, women's rights, the rights of gay and lesbian people, and the rights of people with disabilities have at their cores the issue of human dignity. It has also become the key concept in the worldwide struggle for human rights (Moltmann, 1984). While similar in some ways to the value of equality in terms of relational focus, human dignity is different in that it focuses on individuals rather than groups.

Although B. F. Skinner (1972) is sometimes associated with this concept, many find limitations in his definition of human dignity: the amount of credit that a person receives from others. A broader definition is more widely accepted, one in which a person's intrinsic worth is embedded in human dignity; it involves a person feeling worthy, having a sense of worth, and having others ascribe worth to him or her (Moser, 1973). In this definition of human dignity, all people should be treated with dignity because of their basic worth, and hence all people are entitled to respect and basic rights (Grotesky and Laszlo, 1970).

Human dignity—the acceptance of all human beings as worthy of honor—would seem to be the core of a civilized society. Yet, affronts to human dignity are frequent occurrences, running a gamut from insensitivity to reckless endangerment, to deliberate physical harm. These acts of depersonalization and dehumanization deprive people of dignity (Myers, Laszwell, and Chen, 1980). All too often they are directed at women and at people whose cultures, racial backgrounds, and sexual orientations are different from those of the perpetrators. Sedlacek and Brooks (1976) in part attribute these actions to our inability to understand and cope with people who are different from ourselves, and the results are fear, distrust, dislike, and anger.

Human Dignity as a Campus Concern. Over the past few decades, colleges and universities have struggled to increase the diversity of their student bodies. Court-ordered mandates and moral conscience have led many institutions to improve access for underrepresented populations, a phrase that usually refers to minorities and to women in certain academic disciplines. As demographic declines continue in traditional student populations, and as different minority groups represent larger proportions of the market available, it is reasonable to assume that colleges and universities will continue their efforts to diversify (Levine and Associates, 1989).

As our campuses have become more diverse, there has been a rise in incidents of violence and harassment (Collison, 1987; Magner, 1990). Campuses have sought to prevent such incidents in a variety of ways. They have instituted special programs to enhance awareness of cultural differences, gender differences, as well as differences in sexual orientation. They have instituted curriculum reform, both in terms of cross-cultural course requirements and redesign of existing courses, to be more inclusive. Some have instituted speech codes aimed at barring offensive speech. Although a recent district court ruling declared one code at the University of Wisconsin in violation of First Amendment rights, many institutions continue to rely on such codes (Collison, 1991).

At the heart of the aforementioned court case is the struggle to protect the First Amendment right of free speech, and to simultaneously protect the rights of students to have learning and living environments that are free of harassment. In its report on community on college campuses, the Carnegie Foundation for the Advancement of Teaching (Boyer, 1990) noted two competing elements that need to be present on our campuses. The foundation cited the importance of a just community that honors the sacredness of each person and aggressively pursues diversity, and also the importance of an open community where freedom of expression is protected and civility affirmed.

Challenge for Student Affairs. The challenge for student affairs is to create and facilitate environments that support the diverse needs of all students. This will entail creative programming and attentive response to all actions that place at risk the human dignity of students.

As educators, we must create opportunities for students to understand their differences and to appreciate the richness that diversity affords our college campuses and our lives. In pursuing this goal, we must find ways to meaningfully honor individual identity and subgroup identity without compromising the importance of the identity of the community as a whole. This entails striking a balance between what Levine (1980) characterizes as the two poles of individual ascendancy (where the needs of the individual dominate) and community ascendancy (where the needs of the community dominate).

The effort to affirm human dignity will entail a struggle with our commitment to First Amendment rights and freedom of speech. This struggle is highlighted by Rickard (this volume). Student affairs staff can help their campuses establish reasonable expectations of speech and behavior and carefully educate the campus community and even external constituents, such as nearby residents, parents, and legislators, about the students' rights to free speech and their attendant responsibility for civility. The effort will also require us to guide campuses in their swift and decisive responses to affronts to civility so that all members of our campus communities receive clear and consistent messages about the importance of human dignity.

Altruism

Some scholars report that today's college students value individual achievement over enhancement of the community. They focus on students' concerns for their own vocational aspirations and financial well-being, and their decreased interest in helping others and in being involved in their communities (Levine, 1980; Astin, 1987). Others report that idealism is still a strong, if not always clearly expressed, part of students' identities (Boyer, 1987).

The interest of students in their communities is particularly important at this time because society needs their energy and effort to resolve pressing problems, for example, the plight of the homeless and the deterioration of the environment. These problems transcend individuals and organized governments and require the citizenry to come together to develop solutions (Morse, 1989). Graduates are needed who have an interest in issues beyond self-interest, and who have a profound interest in civic responsibility (Carnegie Commission on Higher Education, 1973). Students must see themselves as part of the "historical procession of humans," whose future is more important than one's limited self-interest (Heath, 1991).

Given the importance of civic responsibility, it is imperative that institutions of higher education prepare students for this responsibility. This is a traditional role of higher education. Brubacher and Rudy (1958) noted that the early American colleges, although educating a small elite group, were preparing students for life roles that included community leadership and good citizenship. Education leaders such as Thomas Jefferson in the early nineteenth century and John Dewey in the early twentieth century reinforced the importance of educating students to be informed and active citizens. More recently, Boyer (1987, p. 218) has recommended student involvement in civic enterprises as a way for students to bridge the gap between "what they learn and how they live," and Lewis (1990) has added self-improvement to the benefits of altruistic acts; people forget their own fears by helping others.

In this time of demanding economic conditions and challenging community problems, higher education will need to find ways to help students make connections between themselves and the community. Student affairs practitioners can serve as facilitators and educators as higher education works to inculcate in students the value of altruism.

Altruism as a Humane Characteristic. Some educators and astute observers of higher education view altruism as a natural human condition and a logical extension of one's humanity. Kolb (1984) believes that human beings have two functional imperatives: the preservation of self and the preservation of the species. He believes that the only dilemma for human beings is to decide the degree of responsibility that they will assume for both.

Implicit in this journey to take responsibility is the struggle between self-interest and the public good (Bellah and others, 1985). The balancing of self-interest and community service characterizes the American tradition. This balancing is particularly challenging for college students since social bonds are tenuous during this period of life for many traditional age students, which makes it particularly difficult for them to come to grips with their interdependence (Boyer, 1990). Other, nontraditional age students are grappling with multiple role demands and the resulting stress (Schlossberg, Lynch, and Chickering, 1989).

The keys to achieving this balance are acknowledgment of the interconnection of self with others and acceptance of the notion that civic responsibility and community service evince both altruism and enlightened self-interest. This new view acknowledges the natural harmony between self-interest and the good of the community (Bellah and others, 1985).

Challenges for Student Affairs. Challenges for student affairs practitioners relate to helping campus communities understand the concept of altruism and its implications for self and society, and to helping individuals and groups find meaningful ways to exercise altruistic values. Some educators have suggested that community service is the vehicle to accomplish these ends. For example, Boyer (1987) has written that a service project on campus or in the community should be an integral part of the undergraduate experience. Others have supported this recommendation and designed models through which community service can become a vehicle for the development and expression of altruism. Through the service learning model—exploration, clarification, realization, activation, and internationalization—students emerge with skills and a commitment to serve. This model helps students apply knowledge through meaningful contributions to their communities (Delve, Mintz, and Stewart, 1990).

To maximize those opportunities, student affairs professionals can assist their institutions in rethinking traditional boundaries between the curricular and extracurricular elements of college life, and between institutions and the communities in which they geographically reside. The breakdown of these boundaries will bring coherence to community service notions as well as to students' general education, both of which are vital if students are to understand themselves in relation to others, and if they are to embrace altruism as an essential priority.

Conclusion

Equality, human dignity, and altruism are values that are inextricably bound together under the umbrella of "care." It is through these values that individuals learn to define and transcend themselves in relation to others.

The role of helping students achieve this end has always been the responsibility of higher education. In characterizing institutions of higher education, Boyer (1990, p. 54) has noted that caring communities help students make the connection between "what they learn and how they live," which makes the college campus not only a "place of introspection, but also a staging ground for action," enabling students to take the knowledge they have gained and apply it to achieve worthwhile ends.

Operationalization of these values is complex, as it involves moral convictions, legal dimensions, and pragmatic needs. It is additionally complex because these values have a delicate interplay with the traditional values of the academy: truth, justice, and freedom (see Rickard, this volume). Adherence to the traditional values of the academy has been perceived as more germane to higher-order thinking than adherence to the caring values, which are frequently linked to feelings and emotions (Canon and Brown, 1985). Gilligan (1982) challenged this perception, however, when she asserted that concerns about human relationships and contextual thinking reflect higher-order cognitive skills. Noddings (1984) suggested that rationality is a positive aim of education, and that it must be seen as contributing to a higher goal, the maintenance and enhancement of caring. This bringing together of rationality and caring is reflected in the work of Noddings (1984), Canon and Brown (1985), and Gilligan (1982). They and others have promulgated a notion of the "ethics of care," in which concern for relationships is a cornerstone for institutions of higher education.

In a community in which the ethics of care is operationalized, the values of equality, altruism, and human dignity assume their appropriate importance. As previously noted, the caring values have always coexisted with the traditional values, but they have taken on new importance in light of the changing demographics of higher education and the changing needs of society. Although traditional values continue to be important, they are enriched by their interplay with the caring values: Truth expands to include new perspectives that equality has helped us to realize, justice is humanized when students realize their responsibilities through altruism, and freedom is tempered by the recognition of the importance of human dignity.

References

American Council on Education. *The Student Personnel Point of View.* American Council on Education Studies, no. 1. Washington, D.C.: American Council on Education, 1937.

American Council on Education. *The Student Personnel Point of View.* American Council on Education Studies, no. 13. Washington, D.C.: American Council on Education, 1949.

Astin, A. W. *The American Freshman: Twenty Year Trends, 1966–1985.* Los Angeles: Higher Education Research Institute, Graduate School of Education, University of California, 1987.

Bellah, R. N., and others. *Habits of the Heart: Individualism and Commitment in American Life.* New York: HarperCollins, 1985.

Bloom, A. *The Closing of the American Mind.* New York: Simon & Schuster, 1987.

Boyer, E. L. *College: The Undergraduate Experience in America.* New York: HarperCollins, 1987.

Boyer, E. L. *Campus Life: In Search of Community.* Princeton, N.J.: Carnegie Foundation for the Advancement of Teaching, 1990.

Browning, D. S. *Generative Man: Psychoanalytic Perspectives.* New York: Delta Books, 1973.

Brubacher, J. S., and Rudy, W. *Higher Education in Transition: An American History.* New York: HarperCollins, 1958.

Burns, E. M., and Ralph, P. L. *World Civilization.* New York: Norton, 1974.

Canon, H. J., and Brown, R. D. (eds.). *Applied Ethics in Student Services.* New Directions for Student Services, no. 30. San Francisco: Jossey-Bass, 1985.

Carnegie Commission on Higher Education. *Purposes and Performance of Higher Education in the United States.* New York: McGraw-Hill, 1973.

Collison, M. "Racial Incidents Worry Campus Officials, Prompt U. of Massachusetts Study." *Chronicle of Higher Education,* Mar. 18, 1987, pp. A28–A29.

Collison, M. "Hate-Speech Code at U. of Wisconsin Voided by Court." *Chronicle of Higher Education,* Oct. 23, 1991, pp. A1, A37.

Delve, C. I., Mintz, S. D., and Stewart, G. M. (eds.). *Community Service as Values Education.* New Directions for Student Services, no. 50. San Francisco: Jossey-Bass, 1990.

D'Souza, D. *Illiberal Education: The Politics of Race and Sex on Campus.* New York: Free Press, 1991.

Fleming, J. *Blacks in College: A Comparative Study of Students' Success in Black and in White Institutions.* San Francisco: Jossey-Bass, 1984.

Giddings, P. *When and Where I Enter: The Impact of Black Women on Race and Sex in America.* New York: Bantam, 1984.

Gilligan, C. *In a Different Voice: Psychological Theory and Women's Development.* Cambridge, Mass.: Harvard University Press, 1982.

Green, M. *Minorities on Campus: A Handbook for Diversity.* Washington, D.C.: American Council on Education, 1989.

Grotesky, R., and Laszlo, E. *Human Dignity: This Century and the Next.* New York: Gordon and Breach Science, 1970.

Hauptman, A. M. "Meeting the Challenge: Doing More with Less in the 90's." *Educational Record,* 1991, 72, 6–13.

Heath, D. H. *Fulfilling Lives: Paths to Maturity and Success.* San Francisco: Jossey-Bass, 1991.

Jordan, M. "Need Blind Admissions Policy at Top Private Colleges Losing Favor to Wealth." *Washington Post,* Apr. 6, 1992, p. 42.

Kolb, D. A. *Experiential Learning: Experience as the Source of Learning and Development.* Englewood Cliffs, N.J.: Prentice Hall, 1984.

Levine, A. *When Dreams and Heroes Died: A Portrait of Today's College Student.* San Francisco: Jossey-Bass, 1980.

Levine, A., and Associates. *Shaping Higher Education's Future: Demographic Realities and Opportunities, 1990–2000.* San Francisco: Jossey-Bass, 1989.

Lewis, H. *A Question of Values: Six Ways We Make the Personal Choices That Shape Our Lives.* New York: HarperCollins, 1990.

McPherson, M. S. "Value Conflicts in American Higher Education." *Journal of Higher Education,* 1983, *54* (3), 243–277.

Magner, N. "Racial Tensions Continue to Erupt on Campuses Despite Efforts to Promote Cultural Diversity." *Chronicle of Higher Education,* June 6, 1990, pp. A36–A39.

Moltmann, J. *On Human Dignity, Political Theology, and Ethics.* Philadelphia: Fortress Press, 1984.

Morse, S. *Renewing Civic Capacity.* ASHE-ERIC Higher Education Reports, no. 8. Washington, D.C.: Association for the Study of Higher Education, 1989.

Moser, L. E. *The Struggle for Human Dignity.* Los Angeles: Nash, 1973.

Myers, M., Laszwell, H. D., and Chen, L. *Human Rights and World Public Order: The Basic Policies of an International Law of Human Dignity.* New Haven, Conn.: Yale University Press, 1980.

Noddings, N. *Caring: A Feminine Approach to Ethics and Moral Education.* Berkeley and Los Angeles: University of California Press, 1984.

Okun, A. M. *Efficiency and Equality: The Big Trade-Off.* Washington, D.C.: Brookings Institute, 1975.

Rawls, J. *A Theory of Justice.* Cambridge, Mass.: Harvard University Press, 1971.

Schlossberg, N. K., Lynch, A. Q., and Chickering, A. W. *Improving Higher Education Environments for Adults: Responsive Programs and Services from Entry to Departure.* San Francisco: Jossey-Bass, 1989.

Sedlacek, W. E., and Brooks, G. C. *Racism in American Education: A Model for Change.* Chicago: Nelson-Hall, 1976.

Skinner, B. F. *Beyond Freedom and Dignity.* New York: Knopf, 1972.

Young, R. B., and Elfrink, V. L. "Essential Values of Student Affairs Work." *Journal of College Student Development,* 1991, 32 (1), 47–55.

LINDA M. CLEMENT is director of undergraduate admissions at the University of Maryland, College Park.

Community is one of the most essential values of our profession and should be developed campuswide among faculty, students, and student affairs colleagues.

Community: The Value of Social Synergy

Dennis C. Roberts

This chapter identifies one of the values of our profession that many in the field may not initially recognize as a value. The creation of community is so important and so obvious to us that we might take it for granted.

The approach in this chapter is to look at the historical roots of the student affairs profession for insight about the value of community. These historical roots provide the beginnings of our definition of the concept. Other contemporary definitions of community are provided that refine this initial definition. For example, Schlossberg's (1989) concepts of marginality and mattering embellish our understanding of the term. Next, the chapter explores how traditions and artifacts influence community and how community can be created among faculty, using Kuh, Schuh, Whitt, and Associates' (1991) model of the "involving college." Then the discussion moves to the challenge of creating community through diversity. Finally, the chapter returns to the student affairs profession and the philosophy on which it was founded. Expansion of campuswide acceptance of the obligations of that philosophy is essential if community is to developed on our campuses.

Beginnings of Community as a Professional Value

In her 1987 interview commemorating the fiftieth anniversary of the publication of *The Student Personnel Point of View* (Roberts, 1988), Esther Lloyd-Jones was asked to identify the essential values of student personnel work. Her first response was, "community, unquestionably." The statement was so direct, so simple, and so immediate that it was startling.

The value of community is elusive in many ways because educators, as well as others, have difficulty grasping the concept. In Lloyd-Jones's (1989, pp. 2–3) opinion, "The condition of community is the binding together of individuals toward a common cause or experience. Individuals both enlarge and restrict their freedoms by joining such a community. But whatever restriction results is far surpassed by the individual's and the group's ability to achieve established goals while at the same time creating mutual support and pride."

This definition is historical and contemporary. Among Lloyd-Jones's contributions in drafting *The Student Personnel Point of View* (American Council on Education, [1937] 1986) was the assertion that student personnel work could only be fulfilled when concerted attention was focused on the environment and the power of students, faculty, and staff working alongside each other in a community setting.

Community as Espoused in *The Student Personnel Point of View*

One of the primary reasons for convening the American Council on Education (ACE) Student Personnel Committee in 1937 was to study and then propose an appropriate way to deal with the emerging role of deans on college campuses of that day. The emergence of these deans coincided with greater pressures on faculty to conduct research and expand the knowledge base of their disciplines; the role of dean had been implemented on a number of campuses to fulfill the duties that faculty members had previously performed outside the traditional classroom.

As Young (this volume, Chapter One) has indicated, a great deal of attention was given to the importance and uniqueness of the individual in *The Student Personnel Point of View*. This focus on the individual was complemented by attention to the environment, but it is clear that most of the references are to the individual and not to the collective community. There may be a variety of reasons why this happened. One likely reason is that community is essentially a feminist concept. When one looks at how *The Student Personnel Point of View* came to be, it is a tribute to Lloyd-Jones, a woman serving on an all-male ACE committee, that the value of community is included at all, let alone espoused prominently.

The feminist values of connecting, working together, and creating a shared reality were evident to Lloyd-Jones when she studied at Columbia University in the late 1920s. She observed faculty and students integrating the disciplines of anthropology, sociology, and theology in ways that illuminated the importance of the environment as it impacted the individual. This experience caused Lloyd-Jones to permanently see the campus in a different way from most of the others around her. The newness of Freudian psychology in America had captured the imagination of many intellectuals, leading them to concentrate on the importance of the individual and an individual's well-being and development. However, Lloyd-Jones asserted that equal value should be placed on the interaction of the individual and the environment. Education and the development of human potential is achieved by attending to the individual, as a whole, within a community. Community is the connection, the support, and the focus of attention that make it possible for the individual to take risks in the education process.

Other Conceptualizations of Community

Because community is so broad and difficult to define, it may be helpful to review two other definitions of community. Boyer (1990) sought to define community by identifying key attributes of a true campus community: (1) educationally *purposeful*; (2) *open*, that is, a place where freedom of expression is uncompromisingly protected and where civility is powerfully affirmed; (3) *just*, that is, a place where the sacredness of the person is honored and where diversity is aggressively pursued; (4) *disciplined*, that is, a place where individuals accepted their obligations to the group and where well-defined governance procedures guide behavior for the common good; (5) *caring*, that is, a place where the well-being of each member is sensitively supported and where service to others is encouraged; and (6) *celebrative*, that is, a place where the heritage of the institution is remembered and where rituals affirming both tradition and change are widely shared. Peck (1987) described a community as both a process and place. Community is something that emerges through the process of interaction, but it is also a place where the individuals comprising the community can communicate honestly with each other, where their relationships are authentic and intimate, and where the members are committed to sharing their joys and their sorrows.

These formulations of community help to expand and enhance the conceptualization of community. They are not really different from the definition provided by Lloyd-Jones (1989); these other definitions simply embellish different perspectives on the same phenomenon. Indeed, the ideas of Lloyd-Jones, Boyer, and Peck can be combined to form a list of essential elements required to establish community:

Common values and resulting purpose
Psychic as well as practical collaboration
Connecting, supporting, and affirming
Openness to question and challenge that respectfully seeks new understanding
Voluntary modification of personal freedoms so that a greater collective good can be achieved
Fulfillment of others' and the community's aspirations.

Institutional Evidence of Community

Seldom can a college or university mission statement be found that does not put forth the "creation of a community of scholars" as a major institutional goal. The words are so frequently used that they really have no purpose in differentiating one institution from another, nor do these words usually compel a college or university to provide explicit programs directed at creating community.

Is community to be found in the winning football team? Is it to be found in a faculty member or student receiving a distinguished award or fellowship? Has a college achieved community when it is selected for listing in a national publication describing the nation's top ten bargains in academe? Is community found among student groups who pursue a common academic, service, social, or other aim? Is community found in the aftermath of a campus tragedy or crisis?

The answer to any of these questions is likely to vary. And it *should* vary depending on how campus students, faculty, and staff relate to any specific happening. What the examples mentioned above have in common is the potential to draw members of the community together for a transcending purpose. These unifying purposes may include celebration, mourning, honoring, or even a focus on creating community.

What makes community such a compelling phenomenon is that, in achieving a goal, both the individual and the organization are benefited beyond what could have been achieved independently of each other. This is social synergy, or what Young and Elfrink (1991) have called the "mutual empowerment" of community.

Social synergy, the adhesive that binds individuals together in community, can be further illustrated through the use of Schlossberg's (1989) concept of mattering, which is actually a continuum of mattering to marginality. Marginality is a feeling of being "out of things," the nagging question of whether or not one belongs. Marginality is a temporary position of passage into or out of an organization; or it may be a more or less permanent condition that results from the community excluding the person for reason of background, appearance, commitment, or other arbitrary factor. Mattering is a motive: the feeling that others depend on us, are interested in us, are concerned with our fate, or experience us as an extension of themselves. Mattering is conveyed through (1) *attention,* or our command of another person's interest or notice; (2) *importance,* or the belief that another person cares about what we think and do or is concerned about our fate; (3) *ego extension,* or the feeling that another person is proud of our accomplishments or saddened by our failures; (4) *dependence,* or the feeling that someone else counts on us; and (5) *appreciation,* or receipt of acknowledgment or reinforcement for our contribution.

Artifacts of Community

The evidence that leads individuals to believe that they do or do not matter is powerfully conveyed through a community's traditions, rituals, and other cultural artifacts. In essence, these artifacts declare what the community is and define which of us do or do not matter to the community. Some traditions on a college campus may be explicit, and many others may be implicit or hidden. Student personnel staff and faculty can impact either the explicit or implicit traditions, but, at minimum, the explicit traditions of the institution should send messages that draw others into the community rather than exclude them. Traditions give either inclusive, community-enhancing messages about the mattering of individuals, or they give exclusive, differentiating messages that make certain people marginal.

Physical locations can give powerful symbolic messages to new members of a college or university community. Is there a place where all members of the campus can join together? Is there a space where people can casually walk, sit, or converse with one another? Many campuses have a mall or a dell. Others have sidewalks that cross paths. The actual physical locations are important, but more important is what the campus members make of these locations. For example, at Lynchburg College, the sidewalks of the campus intersect at the Fellowship Circle, which has a medallion imbedded in the center, commemorating the founding of the Virginia Conference of Christians and Jews at the college during a time when discrimination and exclusion frequently prevailed in the larger community. The Fellowship Circle, thereby, is a place that joins people of different backgrounds and experiences, and it is assumed that all have something unique and important to offer. Similarly, the heart of the campus of Grinnell College is a central site where students, faculty, and staff go to express political or social concerns; if enough people join hands together around this site to make a full circle, the demonstration is considered successful.

The essence of these physical examples is that they reflect the value that all students, faculty, and staff are important. This value is inclusiveness. There are a number of other values that can be reflected in campus activities or organizations. One of the heavily debated issues on many college campuses today is that of hate speech policies versus freedom of speech. In this debate, we see the value of inclusion juxtaposed against one of the most fundamental of democratic freedoms—speaking one's own mind. Another emerging issue is concern over violence and aggression on college campuses. The value explored here is the opportunity or right of students to pursue education without the encroachment of incivility and physical threat. And, finally, the political correctness debate concerns the desire of many institutions to create more hospitable environments for a broader diversity of students. Can hospitable environments for people of diverse backgrounds be established in contexts where only partial knowledge of a diverse range of cultures and worldviews is reflected in the curriculum?

Convocations and commencements are important campus gatherings where the values of a college or university are frequently most visible. The symbolic objects, regalia, special music, and communal sayings provide an opportunity to explicitly remind the community members of the campus heritage. Likewise, new campus members are introduced to these symbols in a way that frequently makes an indelible impression. Convocations and commencements are made all the more powerful because they are usually timed at important points of passage for members of the community. An opening convocation for new students marks one of the most impressionable moments of those connected with a student's four years of college. Parents and family may join their sons, daughters, spouses, and other relatives for a convocation marking the successful completion of the beginning weeks or months of study at college.

It is important that ceremonies or rituals be carefully designed to send inclusive messages to all participants. Insensitivity may allow speakers to inappropriately focus on traditional age, dependent, first-year students, which has the inadvertent effect of excluding transfer students or adult students with spouses and families. The people who are visible at such ceremonial events comprise another important factor; the leaders who are chosen to make remarks at these occasions ideally will represent the broad membership of the campus community or will even more broadly reflect its goals of diversity.

The rite of passage for traditional age students receives a heavy focus at many institutions, but little ritual in passage of adult students is provided. Yes, the addressing of traditional student transitions is probably easier, but just because some students are older does not mean that their passages are any less important or less difficult. If at all possible, events designed to acknowledge the passage experiences of nontraditional adults should be initiated, even if they are only as simple as providing a meeting time during which various types of students are given the opportunity to express what they are experiencing and feeling.

Tradition and ritual can be modified; a campus need not maintain events or places that are destructive to the sense of an inclusive campus community. For example, a campus could establish a faculty, staff, and student task force on traditions, charged to review institutionally explicit and implicit values. Once the values are determined, a process of interviewing and surveying campus members about the events or places that, in their eyes, are traditions could be undertaken. Once these rituals and traditions are identified, the task force could then work to enhance the inclusive traditions and cease to acknowledge or publicly celebrate the exclusive traditions. Imbedded traditions do not die easily; a frontal attack on some campus traditions may fail.

The more effective strategy is simply to ignore these traditions until they cease to exist.

Establishing Community with Faculty

A frequent problem in contemporary times is that the ideal of community may not appear to be highly valued by faculty. This seeming indifference is partially the result of the inherent or acquired skepticism of the life of an intellectual. The self-selection and training of faculty encourage an attitude of questioning and staunch independence that is necessary for the critical analysis of research and theory. However, this proclivity toward skepticism may inhibit efforts to create community.

Faculty may also not value community on the campus because, in many circumstances, the community that is most important to them is the academic discipline. Academic scholars have acquired training and language that, in effect, isolate them from all others who do not possess the same knowledge or jargon. Therefore, the faculty member may lack interest in campus community as a result of personality type, training, and competing loyalties to other communities.

Student affairs staff must learn to recognize faculty reluctance about campus community for what it is and not take rejection personally. To take it personally is to sentence oneself to a life of frustration in academe; the life of the academic is to express disagreement among friend and foe alike.

Involving College Model

Some campuses are better able than others to aspire toward and achieve community. The "involving colleges" study (Kuh, Schuh, Whitt, and Associates, 1991) identifies attributes of campuses that have been more successful than others in this effort. This qualitative study describes a "seamless tapestry" of educational opportunities that draw students, faculty, and staff together in common community pursuit. This seamless tapestry reflects several attributes that enhance student involvement and, therefore, student retention, satisfaction, and graduation:

Institutions that have a clear mission, kept plainly in view, encourage involvement.

Institutions that value and expect student initiative and responsibility encourage involvement.

Institutions that recognize and respond to the total student experience encourage involvement.

Institutions that provide small, "human-scale" environments and multiple subcommunities encourage involvement.

Institutions that value students and take them and their learning seriously encourage involvement.

Institutions that generate a sense of "specialness" encourage involvement.

Kuh, Schuh, Whitt, and Associates (1991) provide both a method for assessing the campus involving culture and a model for the practitioner to look at changes that could be made to improve the involving environment. The more a campus is able to achieve an atmosphere of involvement for all its members, the more a sense of community will be felt by all.

Community Within Diversity

One of the most difficult challenges of the modern-day college or university is finding a workable unity that embraces the profound diversity present on many campuses. If this diversity is not already present, it will likely characterize the vast majority of campuses in the twenty-first century. The early colonial colleges of the United States had very little diversity. Therefore, the establishment of community was made easy at least from the point of view of the shared experiences of faculty and students. However, the diversity of today's and tomorrow's American colleges is mind-boggling. How can community be established within this extreme diversity?

The disintegration of community on college and university campuses is reflected in a recent survey conducted by the Carnegie Foundation for the Advancement of Teaching (1991). This survey indicated that 73 percent of faculty at research universities rank the "sense of community" at their institutions as only fair or poor; this measure improves to a low of 43 percent ranking "sense of community" as fair or poor at liberal arts colleges. Neither figure can be considered admirable. The survey also found that 71 percent of presidents and student affairs officers believed that the most important factor in improving campus life at their institutions was a greater effort to build a stronger sense of community.

Cortes (1991) weaves a discussion of our nation's motto, "e pluribus unum," into an interesting proposition that could help in creating community even within diversity. He says that our society is founded on the balancing act of being many and, simultaneously, of being one. The juxtaposition of these concepts challenges a college campus "to create a climate in which temporary Pluribus isolationism and continuous Unum integration operate in a mutually constructive fashion" (p. 12). This means that colleges need not fear the interest and yearning of like-background students to associate with one another as long as there are community values that are respected and protected, thereby drawing the various individuals and subgroups together for a common purpose.

Campuses vary a great deal in terms of whether or not they work at being a community. Generally, a campus that does not work to be a community will not achieve it. Community is more difficult to achieve the larger the number of students, faculty, and staff and the broader the diversity in the community. But the benefits of working toward a greater sense of community have been repeatedly demonstrated.

Achieving Community Through Professional Work

Many student affairs staffs have worked to create community since the founding of the profession; this is unquestionable and should be celebrated. *The Student Personnel Point of View* (American Council on Education, [1937] 1986) has been used as a mandate that defines the purpose of the student personnel, student services, student development, or student affairs divisions of most campuses. While at face value this choice of mandates seems appropriate and helpful, it has failed in another major way.

The authors of *The Student Personnel Point of View* were educators first; they were prominent members of the American Council on Education. The nineteen members of the committee set out to describe or define the functions that a *campus* needed to fulfill in order to nurture the holistic development of students within the education community. *The Student Personnel Point of View* was intended to be an *institutionwide* philosophy or commitment as opposed to the philosophy of a specialized collection of services and staff on the campus. Perhaps a contributing factor to the isolation of student personnel philosophy from faculty concerns was the enumeration of student personnel services in the 1937 statement. Had the philosophy been independently established and implementation strategies described separately, would our institutions of higher education have grasped the importance of our point of view for the entire institution?

What was intended as an institutional perspective instead came to delimit a territory or organizational unit. This fractured the intent of many of our American educational institutions, the holistic treatment of students. The fracture resulted in the tearing of the "seamless tapestry of educational opportunity" that was the heritage of student personnel and is the current and future promise of a reunited approach to holistic education.

The impact of only student personnel professionals taking *The Student Personnel Point of View* as the charge for their work was that the concern for the whole student in the campus community was driven to the margin of campus life. Concern for holism and community, had *The Student Personnel Point of View* been taken seriously and adopted pervasively, would have been the mandate for the entire campus rather than the specialized student personnel staff.

This issue relates to the potential fulfillment of community in that, with *The Student Personnel Point of View* marginalized, the value of community was also pushed to the margin. The process of community building requires the commitment and attention of all in the campus environs, not just a small band of specialists who serve as an adjunct to the faculty.

The point is that, in many ways, student personnel professionals marginalized themselves. There is not much question that faculty willingly allowed this to happen. After all, faculty attention to research and the advancement of knowledge and teaching could be more easily focused if the demanding and sometimes bothersome out-of-class responsibility for students could be delegated to someone else. In contrast to what has happened, student personnel staff could have been empowered and would have empowered others had they shared the tenets of *The Student Personnel Point of View* more broadly and, thereby, engaged the broader campus in the creation of community.

The days of formation for student personnel are gone. Can student personnel now return, in a new enlightenment, toward the role of fostering community on the campus? Can student personnel philosophy be shared so that all educators, faculty, staff, and students become agents in support of community? Indeed, will there be the rediscovery of self and the healing of a yearning for community for which so many cries are heard today?

Conclusion

In a recent attempt to describe community and help the world find ways to reach it, John Gardner (1991, p. 29) proposed that

> it would be a grave mistake to imagine that—in a great burst of energy— we can rebuild our communities and then turn to other tasks. That assumes a degree of stability we once knew but may never see again in our lifetime. We can never stop rebuilding.
>
> The communities we build today may eventually be eroded or torn apart by the crosscurrents of contemporary life. Then we rebuild. We can't know all the forms community will take, but we know what values and the kinds of supporting structures we want to preserve. We are a community building species. We might become remarkably ingenious at creating new forms of community for a swiftly changing world.

Although written for a broader audience than student personnel workers or even educators, this description appears to be our challenge. We are, indeed, a "community-building species" with a contribution to make. Community making is our heritage, and now we must attempt to find ways to fulfill the vision that has been ours from the inception of student personnel work.

References

American Council on Education. "The Student Personnel Point of View." In G. Saddlemire and A. Rentz (eds.), *Student Affairs: A Profession's Heritage.* Media Publication No. 40. Alexandria, Va.: American College Personnel Association, 1986. (Originally published 1937.)

Boyer, E. L. *Campus Life: In Search of Community.* Princeton, N.J.: Carnegie Foundation for the Advancement of Teaching, 1990.

Carnegie Foundation for the Advancement of Teaching. "Perspectives on Campus Life." *Change,* 1991, *23* (5), 21–24.

Cortes, C. "Pluribus and Unum." *Change,* 1991, *23* (5), 8–13.

Gardner, J. *Building Community.* Unpublished manuscript, Leadership Studies Program of INDEPENDENT SECTOR, 1991.

Kuh, G. D., Schuh, J. H., Whitt, E. J., and Associates. *Involving Colleges: Successful Approaches to Fostering Student Learning and Development Outside the Classroom.* San Francisco: Jossey-Bass, 1991.

Lloyd-Jones, E. "Foreword." In D. C. Roberts (ed.), *Designing Campus Activities to Foster a Sense of Community.* New Directions for Student Services, no. 48. San Francisco: Jossey-Bass, 1989.

Peck, M. *The Different Drum: Community-Making and Peace.* New York: Simon & Schuster, 1987.

Roberts, D. C. *Esther Lloyd-Jones's Perspectives on the Student Personnel Point of View, 1937–87.* American College Personnel Association Generativity Project. Alexandria, Va.: American College Personnel Association, 1988.

Schlossberg, N. K. "Marginality and Mattering: Key Issues in Building Community." In D. C. Roberts (ed.), *Designing Campus Activities to Foster a Sense of Community.* New Directions for Student Services, no. 48. San Francisco: Jossey-Bass, 1989.

Young, R. B., and Elfrink, V. L. "Essential Values of Student Affairs Work." *Journal of College Student Development,* 1991, *32* (1), 47–55.

DENNIS C. ROBERTS *is dean of students at Lynchburg College, Lynchburg, Virginia.*

Aesthetic perception provides an alternative way of thinking about student development, cultural diversity, and the assessment of programs. Aesthetic expression adds passion and vision to student affairs leadership.

The Essence of Aesthetics

Robert B. Young

The title of this chapter is taken from Croce (1921), *The Essence of Aesthetics*. It presumes too much. No single chapter can deliver the essence of anything, much less the core ideas of a complex philosophy such as aesthetics. Still, writing it is worth a try. Aesthetics is more essential to our practice than we acknowledge; it needs to be discussed.

The discussion in this chapter begins with the historical role of aesthetics in higher education and student affairs. It shifts to the definition of aesthetics and then turns toward the roles of aesthetic perception and expression in student affairs. Aesthetic perception is more than emotion; it is emotion integrated with cognition. This perception is related to student development, our perceptions of the uniqueness of students, and contextual thinking; aesthetics can improve assessment and cultural diversity. Aesthetic expression brings passion and intuition to our leadership. It comes naturally to us and we should use it more.

Aesthetics as an Essential Value

My review of values in Chapter One of this volume showed that aesthetics was not considered essential in the early days of student affairs. Even more doubt might be raised today. Few respondents to the Young and Elfrink (1991) survey had anything to say about aesthetics. All but four agreed that it was an essential value, but most might have echoed the words of one respondent: "I'm not sure about it, but keep it in."

Such opinions seem charitable next to others. Brubacher (1962) argued that aesthetics has always been criticized by philistines, puritans, and professors. His philistines are among the most prominent critics today: "The

47

arts, the Philistine is likely to say, bake no bread; the arts meet no payrolls; the arts make no direct contribution to the practical, pecuniary life of our economy" (p. 469). Puritans equate aesthetics with decadence (Barnet, Berman, and Burton, 1960); the arts are not only idle, they are immoral. Professors are positivists. They correlate the growth of intelligence with the method of science. Even in modern philosophy, aesthetics has been superseded by scientific analysis and specialized inquiry (Gudel and Melville, 1980).

The effeteness of art for art's sake, the hedonism of art for pleasure's sake, and the anti-intellectualism of art for emotion's sake make the value of aesthetics easy to dismiss. Even faculty (Skaggs, 1987) and academic department chairs (Withers, 1992) in liberal arts colleges rank aesthetics as their lowest current work value, raising questions about the status of this value in even the bastion of general education.

Aesthetics should undergird general education. Brubacher (1965, p. 44) asserts that the "ultimate motive power for [general] studies lies in the consuming sense of aesthetic value," but he acknowledges that aesthetics has been underrated as a component of liberal learning. Ben-David (1972) agrees that people who have received general education should be aesthetically "superior" to others because they have a sensibility for beauty that those people do not have. Kuh, Shedd, and Whitt (1987) concur with both authors that the ultimate goals of liberal education include the development of aesthetic sensibilities. They argue further that these goals are compatible with the aims of student affairs.

Aesthetics has been linked with the most important historical value of student affairs, individual human dignity. The philosophy of *The Student Personnel Point of View* links "creative imagination" (American Council on Education, [1937] 1986a, p. 76) to the self-realization of students. David Drum (1980), a more contemporary theorist, promotes "the aesthetic" as a specific area of student development. He proposes that students should move from instilled aesthetic preferences to independent assessments and pursuits of beauty during their college years (see Hurst, 1987).

Problems in Understanding Aesthetics

Sircello (1980) says that philosophers, artists, and critics have so many conflicting ideas about aesthetics that any discussion of its nature is filled with conflict and confusion. It seems easier for philosophers to take a dialectical approach to the definition of aesthetics, concurring with Croce (1921) that it is *not* ethics or economics or psychology or logic, but disagreeing about what it *is*.

Aesthetics is always related to the arts, and thus the terms *aesthetics, the arts,* and *art* are often used synonymously, but that does not provide much help in understanding its particular nature. Many would agree that aesthetics is the branch of philosophy dealing with art and beauty (Benet, 1965) but disagree on the specific characteristics of that philosophy. Definitions of aesthetics range from the appreciation of beauty to the science of symbolic expression (Cassirer, 1955). Aesthetics is defined by Young and Elfrink (1991, p. 54) as "qualities of objects, events, and persons that provide satisfaction," and that definition does not carry the weight that Stott (1983) puts on aesthetics. He says that the purpose of aesthetics is to integrate, synthesize, and correct the kinds of reductive specialization that work against the aims of the liberal arts. To Stott, aesthetics speaks of "the beauty and coherence of a realized ideal" (p. 85).

Aesthetics involves the significance, satisfactions, and creation of beauty. At its best, it has a perfection of form that integrates emotion and logic (Langer, 1957). This is its "essence" for student affairs professionals, this integrative attribute that leads to the enhancement of human dignity. Aesthetics confirms subjective participation in the cognitive process. It requires engagement and then inquiry. It provides an alternative philosophy to positivist science, and it provides an alternative philosophy for student affairs practice.

This chapter focuses on two components of aesthetics, perception and expression. The first component involves the nature and role of artistic appreciation in student affairs. It extends to the perception of students and campuses as art. The latter component concerns artistry itself. It involves the passion and vision of student affairs administration.

Aesthetic Perception

O indispensable books! O comforting alternative worlds, where all discords are finally resolved, if not by philosophy, then by art—how without you should we reconcile ourselves to this troublesome actual world?

—Edmund Wilson (1952, p. 713)

The Young and Elfrink (1991) definition of aesthetics was borrowed from the American Association of Colleges of Nursing (1986), which included aesthetics among its essential values of professional nursing education. The definition focuses on aesthetic perception, for example, viewing a painting or listening to music. It involves beauty and satisfaction.

Prizing Beauty. Aesthetics concerns the appreciation of beauty (Krishnamurti, 1985). This is also a goal of some student affairs practices. Through art exhibits in the union, dance troupes in the theater, and even the college viewbook in the hands of prospective students, student affairs professionals try to get people to appreciate beauty. We expose students to the fine arts as well as the popular arts in order to build their aesthetic experiences and perceptual capacities. Croce (1921) says that beauty is nothing but the precision of an image expressed. By exposing students to diverse and precise forms of the arts, we enhance their overall development (Hurst, 1987).

Satisfaction. When people perceive beauty, they experience satisfactions ranging from sensual pleasure to intellectual appreciation. Young and Elfrink (1991) focused on the satisfactions of students and student affairs professionals in their research on the value of aesthetics in student affairs practice. They attached the following examples of professional behaviors to aesthetics: "tries to make the campus environment *pleasing* (emphasis added) to the student"; "creates a *pleasant* (emphasis added) work environment for self and others"; and "presents self and programs in a manner that promotes a *positive* (emphasis added) image of student affairs work" (p. 52). The respondents in their survey were asked to modify these behaviors or suggest alternatives to them, but none did. The respondents seemed to accept a link between satisfaction and aesthetics in student affairs.

The concept of satisfaction is troubling to some, especially when it involves the pleasure principle. Some "puritans" (Brubacher, 1962) find hedonism in any pleasure and abundant examples of hedonism on every college campus: intemperate drinking, graffiti, and date rape. Lewis (1990) is not the only person who places the aesthete among such advocates of prodigal values as the naif, the escapist, the profligate, and the decadent. Such opinions about aesthetics caused Croce (1921) to expend great energy trying to isolate hedonistic pleasure in a narrow corner of this broad philosophy.

Aesthetic satisfaction is more than pleasure. The books that inspired Wilson (1952) are not all pleasure-filled fantasies. They include the Shakespearean histories with their murders and mayhem. Many of the satisfactions of beauty are neither pleasurable nor sensate (Croce, 1921).

What gives distinctive satisfaction in art, music, literature, or other aesthetic activities? Emotion. In Sanskrit, the word *rasa* means the mood or sentiment that is evoked by a work of art. Literally, it refers to the essential oils of a fruit or the perfume of a flower. It is used to capture the emotional essence of art when other words are inadequate (Rheingold, 1988). Goodman (1980) says that the distinction between the scientific and the aesthetic is somehow rooted in the difference between knowing and feeling; it is between the cognitive and the emotive.

But it is more than that. Aesthetics is emotion framed. Goodman (1980, p. 311) states, "In aesthetic experience the emotions function cognitively." The emotions are felt and then cognition discriminates and relates them in order to "gauge and grasp the work and integrate it with the rest of our experience" (p. 311). The satisfaction is integrated and organized and not merely indulged. As T. S. Eliot said, the poet expresses the emotional equivalent of thought. The result of that expression is a unity unachievable without aesthetic sensibilities. Perhaps that is the reason why Emily Dickinson said that Beauty and Truth were brethren, they were kinsmen, and John Keats claimed that they were one and the same.

Goodman (1980) contends that aesthetic perception includes the cognitive recognition of density, repleteness, and exemplification. Density involves the number and order of symbols within a scheme, the comprehension of a system; repleteness concerns the comprehensiveness of features in a scheme; and exemplification refers to illustrations of meanings: These are holistic aesthetic components, not linear scientific attributes.

These ideas about aesthetic perception can be useful to our profession. The discussion turns now to the role of managing emotions in student development, the perception of individual students as art, and the perception of contexts, particularly in regard to cultural diversity.

Aesthetics and Managing Emotions

> Perhaps that which differentiates [humans] from other animals is feeling rather than reason. More often I have seen a cat reason than laugh or weep. Perhaps it weeps or laughs inwardly—but then perhaps also inwardly, the crab resolves equations of the second degree.
>
> —Miguel de Unamuno (1963, p. 2)

De Unamuno regarded emotions as the most important attribute of human beings, and thus he considered them to be the most important concern of philosophy. Aesthetics is the philosophy that involves emotions and it can help us develop the capacities of students in this realm.

Chickering's second vector of college student development "involves increasing awareness of one's feelings and integration of feelings which allows flexible control and expression" (Widick, Parker, and Knefelkamp, 1978, p. 22). Student affairs professionals have always tried to guide the emotional development of students (American Council on Education, [1949] 1986b). We deal with their issues of sex and aggression every day. Students have other emotions as well, and the study of art enlarges feelings; it does not simply confirm them (Barnet, 1989). Increased numbers of aesthetic activities in student unions and residence halls could expand the recognition and discussion of feelings by students, but these activities must be developed by individuals who can enhance students' comprehension of the density, repleteness, and exemplification of emotions. Increased and improved aesthetic experiences in courses and seminars would help, too. The classroom must acknowledge students' emotional fabric as well as their mental fiber.

It might be noted, however, that Chickering (1969) makes just a brief reference to the role of aesthetics in emotion management. He notes that the "creative process requires similar confrontation of emotions [to aesthetics], enables similar legitimate expressions of feelings. Watch the child of an angry mother try to draw a friendly woman. Warm smiles become toothy grimaces or fanged snarls; soft hands become crooked claws; casual posture becomes a fixed stance" (p. 30). These words appear in the middle of a discussion about the development of physical and manual competence, part of Chickering's first vector of student development. Chickering adds that the arts offer a sense of accomplishment that "interact[s] with intellectual competence and the development of identity" (p. 30). In what might be the only other discussion of aesthetics and student development, Drum (1980) describes a continuum of aesthetic development from instilled preferences through broadened appreciation to enhanced sensitivity (see Hurst, 1987). Drum defines "enhanced sensitivity" as a personalized image of beauty, but his primary interest lies more in the development of autonomous aesthetic sensitivities than with the makeup of those sensitivities.

It is possible that all three interpretations of the impact of aesthetics are appropriate and somewhat related; using Chickering's scheme, that aesthetics involves his first through fourth vectors: developing competence, managing emotions, becoming autonomous, and developing identity. If so, then it might be especially important for student affairs professionals to promote aesthetic involvements during the freshman and sophomore years, since there is some correlation between a student's first years in college and work on the first vectors of student development (Rodgers, 1989).

Students as Art

Why do the words *students as art* look strange? *The Student Personnel Point of View* (American Council on Education, [1937] 1986a) describes student affairs as one of the most important efforts of American education to treat students as individuals, rather than as entries in an impersonal roster. Why not, then, as art? That treatment enhances their uniqueness and provides clues for finding more information about their characteristics.

The uniqueness of students gets lost when they are considered only as enrollment data, cultural groups, or psychological vectors. Students become reproductions just as Mona Lisas are reproducible on tee shirts. The context and meaning of the original gets lost: "Each image reproduced has become part of an argument which has little or nothing to do with the painting's original independent meaning" (Berger, 1972, p. 28). The preeminent historical value of student affairs is individual human dignity. The student has importance as an original work of art and not just as one of many reproductions.

This frame of reference leads to a conception of student affairs professionals as critics of the arts. They would not just operate as behavioral scientists who determine the values-neutral commonalities that explain the attitudes and conduct of students. Instead, they would find in students as art objects "qualities in which the great world and its parts seem often wanting: human significance, human order, reason, mind, causality, boundary, harmony, perfection, coherence, purity, purpose, and permanence" (Dillard, 1982, p. 176), "but only if we first consider the raw world as a text, as a meaningful, purposefully fashioned creation, as a work of art" (p. 144).

Counselors are accustomed to interpreting the nonverbal behaviors of their student clients. Do they see all of the art of their students, those portraits and sculptures with their compositions, shapes, contour lines, diagonals, depth, hues, light, scale, poses, drapery, and facture? The last term, facture, means the effect of tools on a sculpture (Barnet, 1989). The facture of each student should change as he or she enters, stays, and leaves college. We should see the lines, the abrasions, and the impact of our brush strokes on students.

The whole picture is more than the sum of its parts, so too is the student. Matisse said, "The whole arrangement of my picture is expressive. The place occupied by figures or objects, the empty spaces around them, the proportions, everything plays a part" (Barnet, 1989, p. 21). Aesthetic appreciation helps student affairs counselors and administrators to understand the wholeness of their students. For example, if a student were to walk into the student affairs office wearing a sweatshirt with a political slogan on it, do we see only the words on the sweatshirt or do we perceive the slogan through the individual student: why she bought the sweatshirt; why she has a closet full of clothes with slogans on them; the impact of this slogan on her roommate, her professor of psychology, and her sorority; her parents' control of her politics; or maybe that this sweatshirt was the only clean piece of blue clothing she had to wear today and she wanted to wear something blue? Aesthetics puts the full student into our consciousness; it makes us perceive the density, repleteness, and exemplifications of her clothing statements and thus her uniqueness as an individual.

Aesthetic Perception and Contextual Thinking

Aesthetic perceptions differ from scientific ones. This, more than any other characteristic, has diminished the status of aesthetics within the academy. Cowley (1961) stated that colleges and universities, more than any other Western institutions, uphold the values of science, of analytical knowledge. He distinguished analytical knowledge from poetic knowledge, the "knowledge gained through imaginative thinking, intuition, revelation, or other non-analytic means" (p. 128). Poetic knowledge was "anti-intellectual"; it might be acceptable in the domains of poets and clerics, but not in the domain of professors. Cowley cited the damnation of science by "poets, professors of literature, painters, and others" (p. 131), and he alleged that their anti-intellectualism had slowed the acceptance of the fine arts in the academy more than any vestiges of puritanism. However, Cowley seemed to believe that aesthetics was as important as science to colleges and universities, though, as Hans Zimsser observed, these "currents of modern thought continue to flow separately, side by side, rarely finding the same channels" (Cowley, 1961, p. 132).

In the aesthetic, context has meaning. Good art engages the viewer, bad art does not (Dillard, 1982). The viewer does not just see something or think about something, he or she experiences it (Barnet, 1989). Classical scientific inquiry separates the viewer from the viewed. The context is removed as well as the participation.

Goodman (1980) compares aesthetic and scientific methods of inquiry. Both involve the invention and processing of symbols, but density, repleteness, and exemplification are the earmarks of the aesthetic while articulateness, attenuation, and denotation are earmarks of the scientific. Goodman's analysis of aesthetics and science echoes recent discussions of feminist and masculine psychologies and of African and Eurocentric mentalities. The aesthetic, feminist, and African modes of inquiry focus on relationships, while the scientific, masculine, and European modes focus on independence. Both involve cognition but in alternative ways.

Aesthetics enhances our appreciation of the cultural environments of our colleges and universities, of our campuses as art. For example, student affairs professionals analyze the psychological and statistical composition of residence halls, but not their aesthetic composition. Density involves the number and arrangement of symbols. How are the students arranged in Hall X? Are all the seniors on the top floor and the freshmen on the bottom? Do the athletes have their own hall? Is it the newest one on campus? What does that say about a campus? Repleteness shows that the picture is complete. Is there something missing from the picture of the residence halls on the north side of a campus? Or maybe the discipline system is not comprehensive because the area coordinators are not involved in it. Exemplification is the symbolic strength of the canvas/campus. It is often applied in counseling through metaphorical analysis. By approaching personal problems obliquely, their factual nature might be revealed. It is also useful in residence life. Every system has its "jungle" and its "geek house." The informal identities of these residence halls mean more to students than the formal names above the doors. If we were to ask commuting students on the Kent State campus where Prentice Hall is, most of them would not be able to tell us. But if we ask them where the students got shot by National Guard troopers, they will point toward Prentice Hall. Since every campus has its own symbols, it becomes our obligation to understand their strength and how they affect students.

Aesthetics provides a common ground where diverse forms of inquiry might meet: in student centers, residence halls, and classrooms. It is not tainted by identification with any particular cultural group or with any single sex; aesthetics belongs to everyone. It celebrates cultural diversity by celebrating the beauty of diverse clothing, the food, the dances, the crafts, and the "different voices" of different people. Exposure to aesthetics advances an alternative way of thinking as well as the satisfactions that can come from encountering diversity.

"Philosophy lies closer to poetry than to science" (De Unamuno, 1963, p. 2), and the holistic conceptions of student affairs are more connected to aesthetics than to classical science. Beauty involves the integration of feeling and reason. Beauty is unity; "ugliness is fragmentation" (Krishnamurti, 1985). Aesthetic appreciation is connected to the perceiver of beauty. It is not linear, it is lyrical (Croce, 1921). Aesthetics enables students to understand their emotions, appreciate diversity, and thus come closer to wholeness. Those who advocate holistic education must advocate aesthetics. Student affairs professionals must enhance the aesthetic experience of students, they must perceive students and the campus in aesthetic ways, and they must increase the art of their administration through aesthetic expression.

Aesthetic Expression

> Art lacks the thought that is necessary ere it can become myth and religion, and the faith that is born of thought; the artist neither believes nor disbelieves his image; he produces it.

> —Benedetto Croce (1921, p. 18)

The experience of art requires someone's expression of it. It is not an idea without an object: "An aspiration enclosed in the circle of a representation— that is art" (Croce, 1921, p. 30).

Aesthetics expressed is beauty created. The three professional behavior examples in the Young and Elfrink (1991) research imply some level of aesthetic expression. "Making the campus environment pleasing to the student" could involve cultural programs, art exhibits, and the physical upkeep of residence halls and student unions. "Creating a pleasant work environment for self and others" and "presents self and programs in a manner that promotes a positive image of student affairs" extend aesthetic expressions to professionals as well as students.

The *product* of artistic expression is important. The *process* of expression might be even more important to student affairs professionals (Council of Student Personnel Associations, [1972] 1986). Aesthetics provides the foundation for the "art" of student affairs administration, which Borelli (1984, p. 14) described as the blending of technical skills with vision: "Artists use vision and passion to realize their crafts and to communicate and create a response in others. Managers use imagination and daring to redesign their organizations and the vision they create to inspire others to share it as their own." Croce (1921) would have agreed that art requires the expression of an image born of passion and composed through intuition.

Passion and Intuition

The emotional aspect of art has been described earlier; the term passion raises its intensity. The term makes some managers uncomfortable, just as the sexual and aggressive passions of students make our jobs more difficult. But the profession of student affairs has always held the point of view that students need to develop their emotions, faith, and values—the stuff of passion as much as the stuff of intellect. We should express that point of view passionately but not just emotionally. Aesthetic expression "preserves the intuitive force, owing to which judgments come forth expressed together with the passionateness that surrounds them, and therefore, they retain their artistic . . . character" (Croce, 1921, p. 76). The expression of feeling is composed by intuition, which Borelli (1984) labeled vision.

Croce (1921, p. 8) summarized his opinions about aesthetics "in the simplest manner, that art is vision or intuition." Vision is overworked in popular management primers, but it has not been related to aesthetics, which equates vision with intuition. Vision as artistic intuition is connected to emotion as much as to intellect. It is the "third part of the mind" that links the primitive brain (emotions) with the conscious mind: "Hence, most creative discoveries are intuitively derived and only later 'dressed up' by logic, observation, or some other conscious technique" (Lewis, 1990, p. 138). Student affairs administrators should be aesthetic leaders. Aesthetic leadership allows us to rely on our total perceptions of the university environment. It allows us our emotions, their depth and their breadth, and our intellect to organize them. We teach students how to manage their emotions. Aesthetics reminds us to lead with ours.

Summary of Practice Implications

While most of this discussion has concerned the philosophical relationships between aesthetics and student affairs administration, I am reminded of the axiom that it is action and not insight that is ultimately therapeutic. Our profession might benefit more by using aesthetics than by discussing it. The following are practice implications of aesthetics that have been raised in this chapter.

1. Aesthetics are tied to liberal education and thus to the classical purposes of higher education; the skillful student affairs administrator will make this connection within the division, with academicians, and with cabinet officers when explaining the importance of our work.

2. We have always had aesthetics management responsibilities. Through art exhibits, clean residence halls, and the college viewbook, student affairs professionals maintain and promote the beauty of the campus. This affects

enrollment management, campus relations, and student development. We need to understand and emphasize the importance of our aesthetics management role.

3. Chickering's (1969) first four vectors of student development—developing competence, managing emotions, becoming autonomous, and developing identity—involve the aesthetic development of students. Student affairs professionals should create more programs to develop aesthetic perceptions, especially among freshman and sophomore students, and publicize the developmental purposes of these programs to faculty and academic administrators.

4. We can become leaders in the assessment movement—nationally and at our own institutions—by using aesthetics to assess demographics, facilities, and programs. For example, residential life patterns could be analyzed according to the density, repleteness, and exemplification of students in the halls. A "portrait" of people, programs, and facilities could be drawn and then room and hall assignments modified to improve the residential life system and, ultimately, stimulate the development of a holistic campus environment.

5. The perception of students as art improves counseling. Aesthetics reminds world-weary student affairs professionals of the uniqueness of these individuals and it promotes the use of techniques such as metaphorical analysis in the counseling relationship.

6. Aesthetics provides a unique way to improve cultural diversity on campus, both through explicit activities and through aesthetic analysis, for example, density, repleteness, and exemplification. Aesthetics belongs to no single cultural group, gender, or academic cohort. We can use it to enhance, justify, and gain acceptance for our cultural diversity efforts in student centers, residence halls, and classrooms.

7. Aesthetics makes up the "art" of good administration, which Borelli (1984) described as the blending of technical skills with vision. Aesthetics justifies the passion and intuition that are part of our work. It organizes emotion with intellect. While this aspect of aesthetics is not tangible, it is absolutely necessary for good practice in student affairs. Aesthetics teaches us how to show that we care.

Conclusion

It was stated earlier that the essence of aesthetics lies in its integration of emotion and intellect and thus in its enhancement of human dignity. Aesthetics confirms subjective participation in the cognitive process. It requires engagement and then inquiry. Aesthetics enables individuals to develop their emotional depth. It enhances the understanding of cultural diversity. It provides an alternative philosophy to positivist science.

Even science is beginning to accept the importance of art. Authors such as Capra (1975) have linked scientists with poets, artists, and novelists. They have described the limitations of classical inquiry and the new acceptance of holism, subjective perceptions, and intuitive understandings by modern science. Space and time are inseparable. One cannot be considered without the other. Therefore, the position of the perceiver has become part of the scientific phenomenon.

Science is getting subjective. As Max Planck has noted, it is coming to mean "the unresting endeavor and progressive development continually toward an aim which the poetic intuition may apprehend but the intellect can never fully grasp" (Zukav, 1990, p. 313). Eventually, aesthetics might become a synonym for accurate science. Today it is an alternative to the limits of logical positivism in the scientific community. Student affairs professionals have always promoted the aesthetic development of students, but they have focused on the functions instead of the philosophy behind those functions. By expanding their understanding of the value of aesthetics, they can increase its possibilities for students, for their profession, and within the academy.

References

American Association of Colleges of Nursing. *Essentials of College and University Education for Nursing: A Working Document*. Washington, D.C.: American Association of Colleges of Nursing, 1986.

American Council on Education. "The Student Personnel Point of View." In G. Saddlemire and A. Rentz (eds.), *Student Affairs: A Profession's Heritage*. Media Publication No. 40. Alexandria, Va.: American College Personnel Association, 1986a. (Originally published 1937.)

American Council on Education. "The Student Personnel Point of View." In G. Saddlemire and A. Rentz (eds.), *Student Affairs: A Profession's Heritage*. Media Publication No. 40. Alexandria, Va.: American College Personnel Association, 1986b. (Originally published 1949.)

Barnet, S. *Writing About Art*. (3rd ed.) New York: HarperCollins, 1989.

Barnet, S., Berman, M., and Burton, W. (eds.). *The Study of Literature: A Handbook of Critical Essays and Terms*. Boston: Little, Brown, 1960.

Ben-David, J. *American Higher Education: Directions Old and New*. New York: McGraw-Hill, 1972.

Benet, W. *The Reader's Encyclopedia*. New York: Crowell, 1965.

Berger, J. *Ways of Seeing*. London: Penguin Books, 1972.

Borelli, F. "The Art of Administration." *NASPA Journal*, 1984, 22 (1), 14–16.

Brubacher, J. S. *Eclectic Philosophy of Education*. Englewood Cliffs, N.J.: Prentice Hall, 1962.

Brubacher, J. S. *Bases for Policy in Higher Education*. New York: McGraw-Hill, 1965.

Capra, F. *The Tao of Physics*. New York: Bantam Books, 1975.

Cassirer, E. *The Philosophy of Symbolic Forms: Language*. New Haven, Conn.: Yale University Press, 1955.

Chickering, A. W. *Education and Identity*. San Francisco: Jossey-Bass, 1969.

Council of Student Personnel Associations. "Student Development Services in Post-Secondary Education." In G. Saddlemire and A. Rentz (eds.), *Student Affairs: A Profession's Heritage*. Media Publication No. 40. Alexandria: American College Personnel Association, 1986. (Originally published 1972.)

Cowley, W. H. *An Overview of American Colleges and Universities*. Unpublished manuscript, Department of History, Stanford University, 1961.

Croce, B. *The Essence of Aesthetics*. Portsmouth, N.H.: Heinemann Educational Books, 1921.

AESTHETICS 59

De Unamuno, M. "The Man of Flesh and Bone." In L. Michel and R. Sewall (eds.), *Tragedy: Modern Essays in Criticism*. Englewood Cliffs, N.J.: Prentice Hall, 1963.

Dillard, A. *Living by Fiction*. New York: HarperCollins, 1982.

Drum, D. "Understanding Student Development." In W. Morrill and J. Hurst (eds.), *Dimensions of Intervention for Student Development*. New York: Wiley, 1980.

Goodman, N. "Art and Authenticity." In M. Philipson and P. Gudel (eds.), *Aesthetics Today*. New York: New American Library, 1980.

Gudel, P., and Melville, S. "Introduction." In M. Philipson and P. Gudel (eds.), *Aesthetics Today*. New York: New American Library, 1980.

Hurst, J. "Student Development and Campus Ecology: A Rapprochement." *NASPA Journal*, 1987, 25 (1), 5–17.

Krishnamurti, J. *Beauty, Pleasure, Sorrow, and Love*. New York: HarperCollins, 1985.

Kuh, G. D., Shedd, J., and Whitt, E. J. "Student Affairs and Liberal Education: Unrecognized (and Unappreciated) Common Law Partners." *Journal of College Student Personnel*, 1987, 28, 252–260.

Langer, S. *Philosophy in a New Key: A Study in the Symbolism of Reason, Rite, and Art*. Cambridge, Mass.: Harvard University Press, 1957.

Lewis, H. *A Question of Values: Six Ways We Make the Personal Choices That Shape Our Lives*. New York: HarperCollins, 1990.

Rheingold, H. *They Have a Word for It*. Los Angeles: Tarcher, 1988.

Rodgers, R. "Student Development." In U. Delworth, G. R. Hanson, and Associates, *Student Services: A Handbook for the Profession*. San Francisco: Jossey-Bass, 1989.

Sircello, G. "Arguing About 'Art.' " In M. Philipson and P. Gudel (eds.), *Aesthetics Today*. New York: New American Library, 1980.

Skaggs, W. "Work Values of Family Members in Selected Small Liberal Arts Colleges: A Comparative Study." Paper presented at the annual meeting of the Association for the Study of Higher Education, Baltimore, November 1987.

Stott, W. "The Role of Student Affairs in Values Education." In M. Collins (ed.), *Teaching Values and Ethics in College*. New Directions for Teaching and Learning, no. 13. San Francisco: Jossey-Bass, 1983.

Widick, C., Parker, C., and Knefelkamp, L. "Arthur Chickering's Vectors of Development." In L. Knefelkamp, C. Widick, and C. Parker (eds.), *Applying New Developmental Findings*. New Directions for Student Services, no. 4. San Francisco: Jossey-Bass, 1978.

Wilson, E. "The Pleasures of Literature." In *The Shores of Light*. New York: Farrar, Straus & Giroux, 1952.

Withers, A. "Perceptions of Academic Department Chairs of Essential Values in Liberal Arts Institutions in Ohio." Unpublished doctoral dissertation, Department of Educational Psychology and Leadership Studies, Kent State University, 1992.

Young, R. B., and Elfrink, V. L. "Essential Values of Student Affairs Work." *Journal of College Student Development*, 1991, 32 (1), 47–55.

Zukav, G. *The Dancing Wu-Li Masters: An Overview of the New Physics*. New York: Bantam, 1990.

ROBERT B. YOUNG is associate professor and leader of the graduate program in higher education and student personnel at Kent State University, Kent, Ohio.

Case studies illustrate how the INVOLVE model can be used to improve the decision-making skills of student affairs professionals within a participatory context.

Values in Decision Making: The INVOLVE Model

Victoria L. Elfrink, LuAnn Linson Coldwell

Scholarly support (Berdie, 1966; Clothier, [1931] 1986; Dalton, 1985; Newton, 1989) for integrating values development activities in higher education exists but, to date, has not been extended to include one of the most basic activities of daily work life, decision making. Our approach is based on the seminal work of Rokeach (1968), who believed that values are the foundation for decision making and mediating human behavior. We propose that the totality of decisions that are made about students links activities and academics across the institution and results in the need for knowledge about resolving value conflicts related to the primary constituencies with whom student affairs professionals work: fellow professionals, students, education institutions, and society (American College Personnel Association, 1989).

In this chapter, we describe the function of values in decision making and link values to current concerns regarding values and participatory decision making within the student affairs profession. A process model called IN-VOLVE is introduced as a means of operationalizing values in the decision-making processes of student affairs practitioners. The description of the model is followed by case studies that show how the INVOLVE model can be applied at several levels within the institution.

Values and Behavior

The term *value* is defined differently by scholars in different fields of learning; however, their definitions are conceptually similar. To illustrate, Kluckhohn (1951, p. 395) described a value as a "conception explicit or implicit, distinctive of an individual or characteristic of a group, of the desirable which influences the selection from available modes, means, and ends of action."

Raths, Harmin, and Simon (1966, p. 38) defined values as "guides to behavior that evolve and mature, . . . are seen as worthy, and give direction to life." Raths, Harmin, and Simon believed that values are chosen freely among alternatives, thoughtfully prized, and acted on. Rokeach (1968, p. 124) stated that a value is "a type of belief, centrally located within one's total belief system, about how one ought or ought not to behave, or about some end-state of existence worthy or not worthy of attaining." Morrill (1980) wrote that values are standards and patterns of choice that guide persons and groups, suggesting that values serve as authorities in the name of which choices are made and action is taken.

A number of authors have distinguished between values and "value indicators" such as attitudes, beliefs, perceptions, and goals. Raths, Harmin, and Simon (1966) said that any concept that does not meet all of the criteria (choosing, prizing, and acting) of valuing is a value indicator. Value indicators, while not considered values, are viewed as potential values since they describe expressions or positions that contain values. For example, Rokeach (1968) postulated that while relationships exist between values and attitudes, the two categories differ in several ways: (1) Values are more dynamic concepts since they have a strong motivational component as well as cognitive, affective, and behavioral components. (2) While attitudes and values are both assumed to be determinants of social behavior, values are a determinant of attitudes as well as of behavior. (3) Attitudes seem to be a specialized concern mainly of psychology and sociology, whereas values have been a center of theoretical attention across many disciplines and thus promote a shared concern for genuine interdisciplinary collaboration. Thus, Rokeach viewed values as more powerful than attitudes, since values determine the opinions and behavior of people.

Many authors have discussed values in terms of their influence on behavior and decision making. For example, Raths, Harmin, and Simon (1966, p. 29) stated that "where we have a value, it shows up in aspects of our living." People without clear sets of values lack direction for their lives and lack criteria for choosing what to do with their time, their energy, and their very being.

Rokeach (1968) concurred with the notion that values affect behavior. He described the following value functions: (1) standards that serve as principles for decision making, (2) motivators of human behavior, and (3) behavioral properties leading to adjustive ego defenses or self-actualization.

Kalish and Collier (1981) wrote about how values and behavior interact when an individual seeks to live a purposeful life. Purposeful living occurs when people seek to live responsibly in their world. Purposeful individuals are characterized as authentic persons seeking both a rich inner life and a healthy awareness of objective reality in their environments. Kalish and Collier believed that individuals develop values to guide and justify behavior in a simultaneous process. According to them, individuals who seek to understand and maintain balance in their environments must examine their values, make decisions, and accept the consequences of those decisions.

In summary, theoreticians have linked values with behavior and decision making. Definitions of the word *value* vary among authors yet seem to center on a means or a method for making decisions in one's life. Values are the critical and central determinants of decision making in human behavior.

Role of Values in Decision Making in Student Affairs

A few noted authors have defined values and discussed their role in student affairs. Kuh and Whitt (1988, p. 23) wrote that "values are beliefs about the importance of certain goals, activities, relationships and feelings." They contended that some values are explicitly articulated and serve "a normative or moral function by guiding members" (p. 23) to make decisions in various situations. Evans (1987) discussed the variety of value-laden decisions that student affairs workers face, ranging from decisions about which formal programs to implement to decisions about how to handle informal contacts with students.

Emerging Values Conflicts in Professional Work

Recent changes in higher education provide fertile ground for the emergence of values conflicts in our work. A values conflict occurs when two or more values arise in a situation, involving two distinct courses of action. The inability to pursue both courses of action at the same time creates a value-laden dilemma and results in the practitioner's need to rank the values and choose one as the guide for decision making and action (Uustal, 1983).

For example, the profession is adjusting to the challenge of serving a more diverse student body with differing needs regarding student development (Levine, 1980). A values conflict could occur when monetary constraints dictate that the chief student affairs officer decide between maintaining an existing orientation program to help all of the students adjust to the university and implementing a new technology program to help disadvantaged students use computers. The requirements of the financial bottom line create values conflicts in the practice of implementing programs and resources for individuals, subcultures, or the entire community.

While the majority of chief student affairs officers and presidents of higher education institutions view the development of more services for nontraditional students as important, the decision to implement particular services involves a knowledge of the environment and a weighing of priorities, values, and goals. Clearly, the effective student affairs practitioner needs to be able to define and articulate personal, divisional, and institutional values and then to be committed to act on them. A knowledgeable choice requires an understanding of the diverse values of all of the participants in the process. This is the basis of the process known as participatory decision making. Participatory decision making, a method used commonly by student affairs practitioners, can be conceptually linked to the processes used to identify and assign priority to the values involved in a particular conflict.

Participatory Decision Making and Values

Many student affairs practitioners have intuitively used the organizational theory framework described by Daft (1989) in which participatory decision making occurs in two major stages: problem identification (the environment and organizational climate are scrutinized to determine if work performance is satisfactory or to analyze the nature of any difficulties) and problem solution (alternatives are considered and one solution implemented).

While participatory decision-making processes entail consideration of multiple perspectives, the values of the participants are not addressed. Only one model of participatory decision making, the Carnegie model, even acknowledges that values influence choice (Daft, 1989). Principally developed by James March (March and Simon, 1958; Cyert and March, 1963), the Carnegie model indicates that the individual values held by managers may contribute to conflict in the decision-making process and that managers need bargaining and conflict resolution skills if values conflicts arise in the decision-making process. The Carnegie model does not, however, describe a means for resolving value-laden conflicts or indicate how managers can determine the values embedded in the conflict. If values are the foundation of decision making, as some experts suggest, there is a need to consider a decision-making model in today's changing world of student affairs work that examines the process of valuing and its role in resolving conflicts.

INVOLVE Model

The INVOLVE model was developed by adapting frameworks from several values development approaches. Kohlberg (1983), Thelen (1987), Glasser (1969), Rogers (1969), Oliver and Shaver (1966), Perry (1970), and Morrill (1980) have addressed some of the instructional and practice-based issues related to making decisions about value-laden dilemmas. While the specific terminology may vary somewhat, each of these theoreticians proposed measures to improve the ability of individuals or groups to make informed decisions by becoming aware of the values involved in complex judgments or choices. The foci of these measures can be summarized as follows:

1. Provide an environment conducive to open discussion between the administrator and staff member (or other parties involved). To illustrate, the administrator should be nonthreatening, the ground rules for discussion should be established, and the administrator should present the notion to the

staff member that the administrator's values are not the focus of the experience.

2. Describe in detail the situation that depicts a value conflict requiring a decision. To illustrate, a situation in which two or more values are in conflict might involve two distinct courses of action for resolution that must be fully explained.

3. Provide time to discuss the decision with an emphasis on the values involved in the choice. To illustrate, the administration should ask the group members involved in the decision to identify the inherent values conflicts.

Use of these three measures results in an informed decision and promotes the personal development of the decision makers. Personal development as it relates to knowledge about values subsequently becomes highly desirable as student affairs officers consider decisions that deal with the complexity of contemporary campus life.

The INVOLVE model uses the above principles for resolving value-laden dilemmas and designing learning activities for values development, in accordance with Morrill's (1980) description of two stages—values assessment and values pedagogy—in the values development process and his notions about designing values development activities for college students. There are three components in values assessment: values analysis (to study values inherent to the situation), values consciousness (awareness of clarification of values in a situation), and values criticism (discover the conflicts or contradictions within the same personal or social system). Once the values assessment has been established, there is a need to develop strategies or practices to transfer the assessment data into the realm of action or decision making. Describing this as values pedagogy, Morrill noted that decision makers must do the following: actively develop and defend their own positions; deeply probe the justification for multiple choices regarding the conflict, but especially for their own positions; confront standards and points of view that are in opposition to their own personal perspective; and assume the role of someone with a contrasting point of view (p. 101). Using this framework, decision makers are challenged to make a decision about an identified values dilemma with an intensified knowledge of the values in conflict, and to further examine the consequence (actions or decisions) related to their values.

In a similar manner, the INVOLVE model focuses on decision makers using interactive means to consider the values involved in a conflict. The basic components of the INVOLVE model are as follows:

I: Include all values that might be *inherent* to this type of conflict.
N: Note the values that define or are important to the conflict of values within this particular personal or social system.
V: View the conflict or contradiction of values within the same personal or social system.

O: Operationalize strategies for conflict resolution within the realm of action.
L: Linger in discussions about views, opinions, perspectives, morality, and values.
V: Vote or make some form of choice regarding the value-laden conflict.
E: Evaluate the consequences of decisions by reflecting on the choices and commitment to further action.

The INVOLVE model is a process model that attempts to have decision makers consider all of the value elements of a conflict. It does not prescribe the outcome or a precise sequence of steps. Several of the steps could happen simultaneously in a group decision.

The INVOLVE model helps decision makers examine a value-laden dilemma in much the same way as a compound microscope helps biologists view an object whose various elements cannot be distinguished by the naked eye. To illustrate further, the basic compound microscope contains two lenses: the objective and the ocular. The objective lens forms a real, inverted, and magnified image of the object, which is then reflected on the ocular lens. The ocular lens adjusts the location of the image so that the eye can resolve detail that is too small to be distinguished otherwise. With the use of these two lenses and a mirror, which reflects the light source, scientists are able to see elements in great detail within the context of a larger organism.

In a similar way, the INVOLVE model uses a set of lenses to create a clearer image of an identified conflict within the context of the decision makers' values. Specifically, decision makers view a conflict through the optical glass of their unique perspectives. The values of the decision makers act as the mirror reflecting two or more opposing choices. Resolution of the dilemma is facilitated by viewing it through the values assessment "lens," which magnifies the conflict so that the values can be separated, the values involved in the opposing choices determined, and possible alternative options described. At the same time that the values assessment lens magnifies and separates the values, a second, values pedagogy lens lets the decision maker view possible choices and their associated consequences within the particular context. Equipped with enhanced perspective, the decision maker chooses—in the terminology of the INVOLVE model, votes on—an action and evaluates the consequences of that decision. An expansion of personal perspective for the decision maker results because of the knowledge gained from defending a choice and assuming the role of someone with a contrasting view.

Application of the Model

We believe that the INVOLVE model can be applied to the spectrum of decisions that student affairs practitioners face daily, helping them to meet the challenges of even the most complex value-laden conflicts. Earlier in this chapter, we noted that there was a need for values development activities related to the decisions that student affairs practitioners make with regard to their various constituencies. Five case studies follow, each representing a value-laden dilemma that holds two or more distinct courses of action. The case studies involve four constituency categories: responsibility to the institution, student learning and development, responsibility to society, and professional responsibility and competence. The case studies are intended to reflect aspects of actual experiences and value-laden dilemmas that have occurred in student affairs practice. Most of these case studies involve residential life, an arena of many values conflicts in student affairs, but not the only one. The case studies do not reflect judgments about residential life or about any individuals or institutions, nor are they meant to provide "correct" answers for each of the value dilemmas. Rather, they are provided to stimulate both application and critical analysis of the INVOLVE model.

Case 1: Responsibility to the Institution. The admissions office is placing pressure on the residence life office to improve the ambience of the residence halls through interior decorating; nonmatriculating applicants have identified the condition of the residence halls as one reason that they chose not to attend the institution. Students residing in the halls do not concur that a decorating change is needed. The current resident assistants state that morale is low and that vandalism and drinking in the halls have increased. The assistant dean of students knows that a reallocation of funds for immediate improvement of the residence halls will result in a loss of funding for other essential service areas such as educational and social programming. The dean of students is also the vice president for enrollment services. What should the assistant dean of students decide to do with the residence halls?

I: Values included as inherent to this situation are (1) truth, or verity of facts in regard to whether or not prospective students are identifying decorating factors or other issues in their choice of institution, (2) aesthetics, or sensitivity to residence halls as in some way not being satisfactory to prospective students; and (3) community, or awareness of how aesthetics and design can affect the development of a positive community within the residence halls.

N: Values noted as related to this specific conflict are truth and aesthetics.

V: Values viewed as in direct conflict are (1) truth, or verity of facts with regard to whether or not aesthetic conditions are impacting prospective student admissions, and (2) aesthetics, or importance of aesthetics in the residence halls for prospective and current students.

O: Assistant dean operationalizes strategies for resolving the conflict within the realm of possible actions: (1) ignore requests for residence hall improvements, (2) meet with admissions office representatives to better understand the specifics of their and prospective students' concerns about the residence halls, (3) meet with current residence hall staff and students to determine their needs and priorities for improvements within the halls, and (4) meet with the development officer to request special capital funds for improvements.

L: Assistant dean lingers in discussion with students, admissions officers, prospective students, and the dean of students. There could be implications with regard to the following: (1) residence halls might truly be aesthetically distasteful to students, thus affecting morale of current students as well as admissions of future students; (2) residence halls might truly be in need of repair, therefore it is possible that vandalism or other acts have increased or have led to disrepair; (3) prospective students may have been concerned not with the aesthetics of the halls but instead with some other aspect of residence hall living; (4) administrators may allocate spending dollars on unneeded decorating improvements, leading students to believe that their college housing dollars are being misspent; (5) residence hall staff may need to conduct several planning meetings to create innovative programming to address issues within halls, especially if programming funds are redirected to renovations and improvements; and (6) current students may have to be relocated if renovations are begun immediately or during the academic year.

V: Assistant dean votes on an action or several actions following lengthy discussions of opposing values and resulting choices. In this instance, the assistant dean decides to form a task force of students, resident assistants, admissions personnel, and alumni to investigate the needs for improvements within the residence halls. It is important to involve the residence halls affected by renovations in prioritizing the improvements.

E: Assistant dean evaluates the consequences of this decision by reflecting on the outcome and making a commitment to further action depending on the task force's actions and student recommendations.

Case 2: Another Instance of Responsibility to the Institution. Students have approached a staff member at a Catholic-affiliated university to do a program on AIDS education. The staff member asks the dean of students about the program, and she says that the program would be fine as long as condoms are not mentioned. Should the staff member conduct the program without mentioning condoms?

I: Values included as inherent to this situation are (1) justice, or fair treatment and exposure of education issues related to AIDS, (2) truth, or verity of facts and issues surrounding AIDS, (3) altruism, or unselfish concern for the welfare of others, and (4) human dignity, or respect for the views of others.

N: Values noted as related to this specific conflict are justice, truth, and human dignity.

V: Values viewed as in direct conflict are (1) truth, or the verity of facts with regard to how the spreading of AIDS through sexual contacts can be prevented through the use of condoms, and (2) justice, or the fairness of the request to limit the exposure of this information in the educational forum.

O: Staff member operationalizes strategies for resolving the conflict within the realm of possible actions: (1) refuse to offer program, (2) do program without a mention of condoms, (3) do program with mention of condoms, and (4) do program off campus.

L: Staff member lingers in discussions of options with other staff members, campus ministry, students, and on- and off-campus health officials.

V: Staff member votes on an option (this can be done by gathering a consensus of opinions, but the ultimate decision in this scenario is made by the individual staff member). In this instance, the staff member refuses to give the program under the current restrictions, explains the situation to students, and explores options of gaining their support to approach the dean of students with an alternative to her expressed point of view.

E: Staff member evaluates the consequence of this decision by gathering feedback from students, campus ministry, and health officials.

Case 3: Student Learning and Development. A residence hall director is rumored to be having a homosexual relationship with a graduate student staff member within his hall. Other graduate student staff members have become aware of the relationship and have gone to the director of residence life to express their concerns about his "morality" and the risk of favoritism by the hall director toward the staff member involved in the relationship. Should the dean of students confront the residence hall director?

I: Values included as inherent to this situation are (1) truth, or verity of allegations and integrity of all parties involved, (2) altruism, or concern for the welfare of all parties involved and concern for student staff posing concerns, (3) human dignity, or respect for others regardless of sexual orientation or cultural and religious perspective, (4) justice, or fair treatment for residence hall director and staff member under policies of institution, and (5) freedom, or unrestricted right of hall director and staff member to maintain a relationship as long as institutional policy has not been breached.

N: Values noted as related to this conflict are equality, altruism, justice, and freedom.

V: Values viewed as in direct conflict are (1) altruism, or concern for all parties involved and the graduate student staff issues of morality and fairness and (2) freedom, or unrestricted right of hall director and staff member to maintain a relationship.

O: Dean operationalizes strategies for resolving the conflict within the realm of possible actions: (1) transfer, fire, or suspend one or both staff members if relationship continues, (2) keep staff members in same job positions if relationship ends, and (3) provide in-service training to staff on issues of homosexuality and bisexuality.

L: Dean lingers in discussions with all parties involved, from graduate and undergraduate student staff members, to other hall directors, administrative staff, legal consul, and the residence hall director and graduate student staff members in question.

V: Dean votes on an action after open discussion of the issue. In this case, the dean chooses to transfer the staff member to another hall and say nothing more about the affair.

E: Dean evaluates the consequences of the action of this decision by eliciting feedback from graduate and undergraduate student staff members, new residence hall director in charge of employing staff member who had the affair, staff member and residence hall director involved in affair, and lesbian, gay, and bisexual student groups.

Case 4: Responsibility to Society. A student puts a large Nazi swastika flag in his residence hall room window, which faces a busy street. The residence hall director has received calls from the rabbi in the community, conveying the anger and hurt of many members of his synagogue. Should the residence hall director ask the student to remove the flag?

I: Values included as inherent to this situation are (1) freedom, or the unrestricted right of the student to decorate his room, (2) aesthetics, or sensitivity to the surrounding environment through display of the flag, and (3) human dignity, or respect for others, in this instance, Jews and others in the community who are offended by the Nazi symbol.

N: Values noted as related to this conflict are freedom, aesthetics, and human dignity.

V: Values viewed as in direct conflict are (1) freedom, or the student's unrestricted right to display the Nazi flag in his room, and (2) human dignity, or the university's respect for its surrounding community.

O: Hall director operationalizes strategies for resolving the conflict within the realm of possible actions: (1) have student talk with local rabbi, (2) ask student to remove the flag, (3) let flag remain, and (4) provide programming in residence halls on the Holocaust.

L: Hall director lingers in discussions about conflict and possible solutions with campus ministry, Jewish students, community, residence hall staff, and the student displaying the flag.

V: After hearing opinions from all involved, hall director votes to ask the student to turn the flag away from the window, but the flag can remain in the room if the student desires.

E: Hall director evaluates consequences of choice through feedback from students, staff, community, and campus ministry.

Case 5: Professional Responsibility and Competence. The new dean of students at a small private college has heard rumors that the directors within the student affairs division were unhappy with the autocratic decision-making style of the previous dean. The new dean believes in involving all affected constituencies in decision-making processes. The college has been experiencing financial difficulties over the past year. The president of the institution recently gave the dean a detailed and itemized proposed budget for the student affairs division for the coming fiscal year. The dean expresses his opinion to the president that the student affairs directors should have input in deciding on their budget priorities rather than have a final budget imposed on them. The president insists that the dean give the directors the budget as she presented it. Should the dean allocate the funds as the president directed?

I: Values included as inherent to this situation are (1) community, or working toward mutual empowerment within the student affairs division as a collaborative and cooperative team, (2) freedom, or capacity for directors to exercise choice in budgeting, and (3) truth, or faithfulness to the institution and the president, and to the student affairs division.

N: Values noted as related to this conflict are community, freedom, and truth.

V: Values viewed as in direct conflict are the division's and the president's respective definitions of community and freedom.

O: Dean operationalizes strategies for resolving the conflict within the realm of possible actions: (1) follow the president's directive, (2) ignore the president's directive and give directors budgetary input, (3) form student focus groups to help set student affairs budget priorities given economic restraints, (4) enlist support of other cabinet-level officers in confronting president's budgeting style, (5) tell president that her directive will be followed but secretly have the student affairs staff create a budget within the guidelines provided, and (6) find ways to increase college income and/or decrease expenditures within the student affairs division.

L: Dean lingers in discussions with directors. There could be implications with regard to the following: (1) low morale among the student affairs staff if they have an imposed specific budget, (2) conflict within the student affairs staff if process of prioritizing budget specifics does not include all available constituencies, and (3) firing or reprimand of the dean if he does not follow the president's directive.

V: Dean votes on an action following lengthy discussions of opposing values and resulting choices. In this case, the dean gathers the directors together to work out budget priorities within the student affairs division given the budget restraints and compares this budget to the plan given by the president.

E: Dean evaluates the budget priorities; if there are severe discrepancies, he will discuss the differences with the president and present the case for changing the funding priorities within the student affairs division.

Conclusion

A great deal of emphasis has been placed in higher education on making decisions solely on the basis of evaluation of empirical data, rather than consideration of the values that exist in each circumstance. A decision becomes particularly difficult when a value-laden conflict occurs. The INVOLVE model proposes a systematic process for analyzing the values embedded in a conflict, thus facilitating an informed choice about the needed action. The model does not prescribe specific values or discount the importance of logical objective data. Instead, it is intended to ground all knowledge within a values structure. Similarly, the model does not describe a lockstep procedure for making choices but rather an interactive process requiring simultaneous reflection and validation throughout the decision-making venture. Finally, the model does not intend to compromise or restrict the diverse views of the parties involved; rather, it illuminates and clarifies the values of those parties.

We believe that the INVOLVE model can be adapted for use in the practice of student affairs both as a framework for decision making and as a means for values development with professionals, paraprofessionals, and students. While the final choice of action remains with the primary decision maker, the model proposes a participative decision-making perspective that has the potential to integrate the views of the constituencies involved in the process of choosing an action. Use of the INVOLVE model can promote a staff's organizational effectiveness through a greater sense of commitment to an institution. An organization that solicits and implements ideas from its members generates greater ownership in the decisions that affect those involved. It enhances the employment experience and promotes the personal and professional development of staff by providing an alternative to traditional rational-objective knowledge, thus sharpening the ability of the individuals and staff team to resolve value-laden conflicts. The resolution of values conflicts is of vital importance to all disciplines within higher education as they strive to make meaningful and informed decisions to prioritize and meet the needs of the greatest number of students. The INVOLVE model can be used to enlighten and improve the resolution of the value-laden dilemmas inherent to the task of providing student services throughout the campus community.

References

American College Personnel Association. *Statement of Ethical Principles and Standards.* Alexandria, Va.: American Association for Counseling and Development, 1989.

Berdie, R. F. "Student Personnel Work: Definition and Redefinition." *Journal of College Student Personnel,* 1966, 7 (3), 131–136.

Clothier, R. C. "College Personnel Principles and Functions." In G. Saddlemire and A. Rentz (eds.), *Student Affairs: A Profession's Heritage.* Media Publication No. 40. Alexandria, Va.: American College Personnel Association, 1986. (Originally published 1931.)

Cyert, R. M., and March, J. G. *A Behavioral Theory of the Firm.* Englewood Cliffs, N.J.: Prentice Hall, 1963.

Daft, R. L. *Organizational Theory and Design.* (3rd ed.) Saint Paul, Minn.: West, 1989.

Dalton, J. C. "Values Education: A New Priority for College Student Development." In J. C. Dalton (ed.), *Promoting Values Development in College Students.* Monograph series No. 4. Washington, D.C.: National Association of Student Personnel Administrators, 1985.

Evans, N. "A Framework for Assisting Student Affairs Staff in Fostering Moral Development." *Journal of Counseling and Development,* 1987, 66, 191–194.

Glasser, W. *Schools Without Failure.* New York: HarperCollins, 1969.

Kalish, R., and Collier, K. *Exploring Human Values.* Pacific Grove, Calif.: Brooks/Cole, 1981.

Kluckhohn, F. R. "Values and Value Orientation in the Theory of Action: An Exploration in Definition and Classification." In T. Parsons and E. Shills (eds.), *Toward a General Theory of Action.* New York: HarperCollins, 1951.

Kohlberg, L. *Moral Stages: A Current Formulation and a Response to Critics.* Basel, N.Y.: Klarger, 1983.

Kuh, G. D., and Whitt, E. J. *The Invisible Tapestry: Culture in American Colleges and Universities.* ASHE-ERIC Higher Education Reports, no. 1. Washington, D.C.: Association for the Study of Higher Education, 1988.

Levine, A. *When Dreams and Heroes Died: A Portrait of Today's College Student.* San Francisco: Jossey-Bass, 1980.

March, J. G., and Simon, H. A. *Organizations.* New York: Wiley, 1958.

Morrill, R. *Teaching Values in College.* San Francisco: Jossey-Bass, 1980.

Newton, F. "A Time to Speak . . . ." *ACPA Developments,* 1989, 16 (1), 16.

Oliver, J. P., and Shaver, D. W. *Teaching Public Issues in the High School.* Boston: Houghton Mifflin, 1966.

Perry, W. *Forms of Intellectual and Ethical Development During the College Years.* Troy, Mo.: Holt, Rinehart & Winston, 1970.

Raths, L., Harmin, M., and Simon, S. *Values and Teaching: Working with Values in the Classroom.* Columbus, Ohio: Merrill, 1966.

Rogers, C. *Freedom to Learn.* Columbus, Ohio: Merrill, 1969.

Rokeach, M. *Beliefs, Attitudes, and Values: A Theory of Organization and Change.* San Francisco: Jossey-Bass, 1968.

Thelen, L. J. "Values Clarification: Science or Nonscience." *Science Education,* 1987, 71 (2), 201–220.

Uustal, D. "Values Education in Baccalaureate Nursing Curricula in the United States." Unpublished doctoral dissertation, Graduate School of Education, University of Massachusetts, 1983.

VICTORIA L. ELFRINK *is assistant professor of nursing at the University of Akron, Akron, Ohio.*

LUANN LINSON COLDWELL *is former director of residential life at Ohio Northern University, Ada.*

Changes in students and the profession make it imperative to teach values to undergraduates and in our preparation programs for student affairs professionals.

The Teaching of Values

Leila V. Moore, Deborah H. Hamilton

Questions about which values we might teach and whether we even have the right to teach values have a familiar ring. We have asked and answered these questions several times during our emergence as a profession. We have deliberated about our responsibility as educators in this sensitive area and have responded differently over the years. The purposes of this chapter are to review our prior approaches to the teaching of values, to discuss the importance of teaching values now, and to suggest how student affairs preparation program curricula can help practitioners to learn how to teach values.

Background

A review of the emergence of values education as a teaching activity at the college level (Raths, Harmin, and Simon, 1978) reveals two core dilemmas. First, the idea of conveying values has typically been surrounded with challenges, such as the morality of teaching certain values and whether this is a role for educators when parents should be responsible for the values education of their children. Second, in terms of the relevance and importance of values education at the college level, it would seem that the very presence of information about values raises concerns about whether the objectivity of scientific inquiry and the discovery of knowledge are somehow compromised. In effect, does values education undermine the purpose and goals of a college education?

The assumptions about what is involved in values education may very well be the basis for challenges such as these. What took place in past values education activities were a clarification and discussion of *values indicators* to see if they were indeed values or if one "wish[ed] to raise them to the value level" (Raths, Harmin, and Simon, 1978, p. 4). Inasmuch as values indicators reflect certain values and not others, one could argue that what a student learns about certain values and not others depends on his or her range of experiences with many values. In spite of a definition of the activities related to values education, critics of values education, particularly at the college level, have argued that the teaching of values is a form of moral persuasion and perhaps even brainwashing that could lead to a return of McCarthyism. With values education activities associated with a fear that college students would not learn to think for themselves and to form their own opinions, those who taught values stressed the clarification aspect of their activities, inferring that their role was simply to show students which values were guiding their own behaviors and to serve only as a mirror of what the students had already learned.

In the past, values education, with or without the definition provided above, has been a peripheral part of the collegiate experience. Its effect on students has seemed to elude measurement and its relevance to the mission of a college or university has seemed questionable. After all, students were entering college with a sense of what they valued, their parents had fulfilled their obligations to provide such education, and colleges could do little to contribute to that process. Discussions about values education, then, seemed to be focused on the inability of those who supported values education to convince others in higher education of the contribution of values clarification activities to the overall education of students.

Changes in Student Values

In the context of the history of higher education during the 1950s and early 1960s, challenges to the importance of the role of values education seemed justifiable. Beginning with the late 1960s, however, some shifts in assumptions about college students emerged. The 1960s and early 1970s saw the assassination of three major inspirational leaders and America's participation in what was to many an unnecessary and immoral war. The literature about those times reflects dismay, a loss of hope, and a crumbling of the importance of dignity, self-respect, and a concern for others. Students began to see themselves as consumers of education, and they began to judge the relevance and importance of their education according to their ability to find a well-paying job after graduation.

The meaninglessness of values that have no relevance to "me" seemed to pervade the student attitudes of the 1970s and early 1980s. For example, Dey, Astin, and Korn (1991, pp. 110–111, 122–123) reported that entering college freshmen in 1985 differed from entering college freshmen in 1971 in these ways: considerably fewer students in 1985 reported that they frequently voted in student elections in high school (64 percent in 1971, 1 percent in 1985), and fewer had discussed politics frequently with classmates (21 percent in 1971, 1 percent in 1985). At the same time, far more 1985 freshmen reported that they often felt depressed and overwhelmed in high school (1 percent in 1971, 16 percent in 1985). More entering freshmen in 1985 than in 1971 labeled themselves as conservative or middle-of-the-road (60 percent in 1971, 75 percent in 1985), more 1985 freshmen considered it very important or essential to be recognized by their colleagues for contributions after graduation (37 percent in 1971, 55 percent in 1985), and far fewer 1985 freshmen reported that it was very important or essential to become involved in programs to clean up the environment (43 percent in 1971, 20 percent in 1985). These data reflect declines in social and political participation, increases in conservatism, a greater sense of helplessness in "making a difference," and a greater need for individual recognition and reward.

Although Dey, Astin, and Korn's (1991) data were gathered from an essentially homogeneous sample of entering freshmen (90 percent were eighteen or nineteen years old and 85 percent were white), the data are our best available indicators of national trends regarding students. Limitations notwithstanding, scholars of the changes in student values indicators from 1960 to 1985 have described the evolution of "the me generation," fully focused on self, determined to get a college education in order to get work that pays more. Notions of altruism, the idea that one selects a college major according to one's interests and abilities, and values such as compassion, a sense of service, and loyalty to one's undergraduate college all seemed to have disappeared since the early 1960s.

Has the student of the 1990s changed at all in terms of values? Dey, Astin, and Korn's (1991, pp. 122–123) data provide mixed information. While there were no changes from 1985 to 1991 in the proportions of students who voted in student elections, discussed politics, felt depressed or overwhelmed, or labeled themselves as conservative or middle-of-the-road, there were changes in other values indicators. For example, more students in 1991 (31.3 percent) reported that it was important to get involved in cleaning up the environment. Slightly more students reported that it was important for them to help promote racial understanding (32 percent in 1985, 33 percent in 1991), and slightly more students reported that it was important for them to influence social values (32.9 percent in 1985, 39.6 percent in 1991).

Who is this newer student? Coupland (1991) describes him or her as a member of "Generation X," a generation that defies characterization. The changes in values such as those reported above may portend a hopeful future for the resurgence of values. On the other hand, the students of Generation X seem to be more diverse in their views, sometimes contradictory in actions that reflect first one value and then its antithesis. The last few years have seen reports of an increasing number of incidents that reflect a diminishment of the values of truth, justice, freedom, altruism, equality, human dignity, community, and aesthetics. A student experiences harassment from others for placing a poster on her residence hall door that contains a quotation from Martin Luther King, Jr. Students mock those who know the words to their alma maters. A community cleanup drive sponsored by a campus service fraternity is canceled due to lack of interest. A campus honor code is eliminated because of increases in the number of cases of cheating. A student attempts suicide because he feels so lonely and unsuccessful in finding friends at school. Oil paintings and watercolors on display in a campus theater and auditorium are ripped and defaced. On the other hand, student volunteerism is up on many campuses, there are more reports of students getting involved in environmental programs, and some campuses report increases in participation in student elections, in charitable fund-raising, and in food and clothing drives.

The contradictions confuse student affairs practitioners, who seek ways to support the positive shifts and other ways to challenge the negative developments. In formulating responses, practitioners are often faced with using techniques and approaches that might have worked in the 1960s but not now with Generation X. What does work? What do we know about today's students and about the values that will help us cope with the contradictory messages that students seem to be sending.

Changes in the Field of Student Affairs

Students have changed during the past thirty years, and both the practice of student affairs and the curricula of our preparation programs have changed in order to keep up. Both the changes in students and the changes in the profession have influenced our view of the role of the essential values of our profession.

In the early 1960s, our field had barely begun to emerge as a profession with a body of knowledge and a set of practices expected of those who were in the field. During this decade, student affairs preparation program curricula included a focus on the individual student and ways in which student affairs professionals might encourage the growth and development of students. Textbooks during those years focused on the concepts of demonstrating unconditional positive regard for students, preserving and transmitting the culture of higher education, and understanding the role of higher education as a reflection of society. There seemed to be an underlying assumption that the matter of values was addressed by helping students to realize that their behaviors and attitudes reflected certain values. The concept of a value-free education suggested that colleges get out of the role of *in loco parentis* and into a more neutral role when working with college students and influencing their values formation.

In the 1970s and into the 1980s, the concepts of person-environment interaction and student development dominated curricula in college student affairs. Our attention turned to the study of the effects of college on students, and methods of scientific inquiry centered primarily on empirical studies and quantitative research. The notion of values clarification seemed to pale in comparison to the notions of moral development and ethical dilemmas. Student affairs practitioners improved their understanding of students and became proficient at applying the theories of the field to the practice of encouraging and supporting the growth and development of students. What could be measured and quantified became the coin of the realm when it came to research about the effects of college on students. Again, values seemed a poor candidate for such research.

As the 1980s ended, there were signs in student affairs preparation programs that the theoretical base on which our profession had relied for nearly thirty years lacked the necessary depth and breadth to help us explain the nature of the college student populations that we were beginning to experience. Shifts toward political conservatism among college students, the diversity in age and ethnicity of the college population nationally, a rise in campus violence, and increased numbers of students entering college with significant family dysfunctions brought into question the utility of the curricula that provided college campuses with student affairs professionals. In the minds of a growing number of recruiters of entry-level student affairs professionals, the complexity of the current scene in higher education was proving to be too much for recent master's graduates to handle effectively.

Student affairs preparation programs have come to a crossroads. The 1990s have brought a student population that is diverse in many ways, there are shifts in our perspective of the campus as a community, and our traditional theoretical base has been labeled monocultural, linear, and narrow in perspective. At the same time, our student affairs graduate students are more culturally diverse, their expectations of graduate education are that they will learn about models and theories that solve current problems in higher education, and, like their predecessors, they expect to make a difference in the development of students.

Teaching Values in Preparation Programs and Elsewhere on Campus

The current problems that our graduate students need to address reflect five shifts in our view of the relevance of values to our work with college students. These five changes are a shift away from a value-free campus climate, a shift away from the sole focus on individual rights, a recognition of the limitations of a monocultural perspective, a growing awareness that policies and rules for students need a major reevaluation, and an increase in the importance of outcomes assessment.

Disappearance of a Value-Free Campus Climate. The disappearance of a value-free campus climate has been accompanied by an increase in the literature of descriptions of campus climates where values are communicated and, indeed, taught. This shift has been prompted by our growing experience with significant social issues of the day. As we cope with increased reports of date rape, for example, how do we leave our views of this social problem at the door when we attend to the student who has been raped, or see the effect of the incident on her friends, or respond to the urgent need for educational efforts directed toward healthy dating relationships? The "caring values" discussed by Clement (this volume) shape those educational efforts. They are reflected in our view of what a healthy relationship looks like, and they guide our assessments of the effectiveness of education programs in reducing the instances of date rape.

Orientation programs are affected by the increased attention to values and the importance of teaching them. Our new students are involved in lengthy meetings and workshops where they learn not just where to find the library but also what the campus climate is like, how to get involved in the life of the campus, and what they can expect from student affairs staff. The value of community influences the design of these programs.

In the same orientation programs, values of truth and justice shape student affairs professionals' presentations on expectations for responsible behavior. Behaviors that are not tolerated are discussed in detail in meetings before the academic year begins. These same values have led more campuses to return to semester-long or year-long programs that both challenge the students' values and beliefs and support the development of a more open approach to people who are different from oneself. The caring values again are reflected in programs where students learn to approach disagreements and arguments in a more rational way, to seek common ground with others as an approach to understanding differences, and to respond in nondefensive ways to challenges to their own beliefs and values.

Shift from a Predominant Focus on Individual Rights. A shift from a predominant focus on individual rights has changed to a focus that also includes acknowledgment of individual and collective responsibility. This change opens the door for the teaching of the essential values of our profession. Wood (1991), for example, calls on student affairs professionals to renew a sense of collegiality on campus. According to Wood, a collegial environment helps campuses to shape communities that contain clearly defined expectations for acceptable behavior; to carry on civil exchanges of opinion among students, faculty, and staff; to repair the fragmentation of community that now exists on campuses; and to encourage faculty to renew their involvement in the life of the campus.

Evidence of the shift toward acknowledgment of individual and collective responsibility is also found in campus administrators' reports of increased instances in which alumni, advisers, and community leaders have asked for greater institutional involvement in holding students both individually and collectively responsible for unwanted behaviors. Student affairs practitioners who wish to respond to these requests will need to understand how to address the consequences of unwanted behaviors, including the effects of such behaviors on others. This understanding can be accomplished through the study of values, their enactment through behavior, and methods of education related to values such as case studies, simulations, role plays, and problem-solving activities.

Limitations of a Monocultural Perspective. Next, as values related to cultural pluralism have become more familiar on college campuses, we have become increasingly aware of the limitations of a monocultural perspective. For example, a multicultural perspective has influenced the replacement of the concept of "either/or" thinking with "both/and" thinking. A multicultural perspective allows us to see students who have been referred to the campus judicial system as both innocent and guilty, as both victim and oppressor, as both right and wrong.

The campus judicial system is also changing to reflect the values of many cultures. Campus officials are encountering many more cases where existing rules and policies fail to guide them to a decision, and where situations pose ethical dilemmas in adjudication. Can both parties be guilty and both be innocent? Are there situations in which to serve justice is to be unfair? Is mediation a better campus vehicle for coming to terms with disagreements? Attempts to respond to questions such as these without a grounding in the values of our profession would place student affairs professionals in the perilous position of responding only from their own personally held values or from the perspective of laws and rules that were written from a monocultural perspective.

Reevaluation of Campus Policies and Rules. The fourth shift involves our policies, rules, and guidelines for students, most of which were written twenty years ago. These policies and rules are in urgent need of reevaluation as we keep in mind the changes in our perspectives about values. Boyer's (1990) discussion of community contains six values on which a campus community must rest. Those values of educational purposefulness, openness, justice, discipline, caring, and celebration must be accommodated in our reevaluation. For example, a policy that prohibits employment discrimination on the basis of gender but is silent about the sexist remarks made by a professor in the classroom surely fails to respond to the values of equality and human dignity as they are carried out in a campus community.

Student affairs preparation programs, through such techniques as case studies and problem solving, can adapt to the importance of teaching values by helping graduate students learn to use the evidence of the existence of values as criteria for evaluating institutional policies and practices. Through such exercises, graduate students can learn to see institutions as systems that communicate values both covertly and overtly, and they can learn to become catalysts for the systemic changes that are needed when institutions send inconsistent messages about the values that are important to them.

Increased Importance of Outcomes Assessment. In the last few years, colleges and universities have paid increased attention to the importance of outcomes assessment. Student affairs professionals, along with other college faculty and staff, have learned to articulate and assess the outcomes of a college education on students. We find ourselves stating those outcomes as things we hope that the student has learned. Often those outcomes statements include such expectations as the student's ability to behave in a moral way, or to resolve ethical dilemmas effectively, or to make a contribution of time and talent in service to others. Outcomes statements such as these are reflections of the essential values of our profession. The parallel between such outcomes statements and the core values is notable and certainly supports the notion that student affairs preparation programs must teach students how to work with those values.

Recent developments in the area of institutional accreditation have also indicated to the field of higher education that accreditation teams may become more systematic in holding institutions accountable for transmitting values. In the future, the quality of the education that a student receives may be measured in part by the possession of attitudes and values related to the student's ability to function as a global citizen. In many institutions, students are already expected to understand the importance of service learning to their role in society. The notion of social responsibility, part of the caring values discussed in Clement (this volume), is finding its way into more campus mission statements and expectations for students. The ability to interact effectively with others and to fulfill leadership roles will have become part of campus recruiters' expectations of their new employees. These abilities are also reflected in the student affairs values about community. Recent discussions about Total Quality Management (TQM) stress the values of teamwork, collaboration, a sense of pride in accomplishment, and a striving toward excellence in service. Students recruited by firms that embrace TQM are expected to behave according to these values. These values, too, reflect the core values of student affairs.

Changes such as those described above have triggered the need for a more systematic examination of our student affairs preparation curricula and whether we are teaching our graduate students how to respond to the shifting values of today's students. The time has come for preparation program faculty to imbed in their curricula the theory and practice related to values. Young and Elfrink (1991) have presented what they believe are the core values of our profession, but what do we do with them and how do we deal with other values that involve undergraduate students with whom we work?

We make the following recommendations for an approach to changes needed in our preparation program curricula:

1. Include in our basic courses the study of the taxonomy of the affective domain (Krathwohl, Bloom, and Masia, 1974) and other models that characterize the stage development of value and belief systems. Teach our graduate students how to develop interventions that help a person move through those stages.
2. Teach the concept of cognitive complexity (Dewey, 1933; Fischer, 1980; Perry, 1970).
3. Teach critical thinking skills (Mezirow and Associates, 1990; Meyers, 1986). Then, teach our graduate students how to teach undergraduates those skills through the cocurriculum. Critical thinking skills, such as identifying assumptions and evaluating the logic of another's thoughts, help undergraduates develop their own value and belief systems.
4. Teach about critical reflection, also known as reflective judgment (Mezirow and Associates, 1990; Kitchener and King, 1981, 1990). Then help our students to practice making moral judgments through case studies and simulations. This experience will translate easily into their work with undergraduates.
5. Include the values differences among cultures in our curricula. In the same manner, introduce the core values of our profession as those that are taught by the "culture" of our profession. Discuss the core values in depth, particularly as they may be reflected in the values of other cultures. Do the core values proposed by Young and Elfrink (1991) reflect the common ground of values across cultures?
6. Teach students how to recognize implied values in the words and be-haviors of others.

As these sources of knowledge, skills, and attitudes are transmitted to our graduate students, they will be prepared to meet the challenges of the contradictory Generation X. They will also be more prepared to deal with the development of a campus community. Many of our students now understand the notion of the campus as community, but many seem frustrated that our efforts to create community have not been successful across a broad array of institutions. Some students ask, "Is the concept of community the exclusive property of small, liberal arts colleges?" We believe that the nature of values has everything to do with how one responds to that question. Community, as Boyer (1990) and Roberts (this volume) describe it, seems to rely on the presence of values. The primary question seems to be, which values should be there? Values that are common to the members of the community are the most likely to survive time and changes in generations of students. These common values may very well be the core values of our profession. As we discover more about the core values and their presence in many cultures, we may discover a way to make a significant contribution to the development of a sense of community on college campuses.

Conclusion

The purposes of this chapter have been to review the history of the definition and role of values education in American colleges and universities and to discuss future definitions and roles for values education. Following the historical review, five recent changes in campus values and practices were identified as major influences on the importance of teaching values now in higher education. Several examples of current incidents and situations confronting student affairs practitioners were used to establish a basis for the argument that we have already begun to act according to the core values of the profession. We have begun to communicate through our recent responses to campus concerns a clearer and more consistent set of values. Because the values that are central to our profession also seem to be the values that have guided most of the recent responses to campus concerns, we are already behaving as communicators of the values of our profession. But we must become more intentional in our efforts to educate undergraduates and our own graduate students about these values.

As for the role of values in the student affairs preparation program curricula, they have emerged already through our discussions of case studies, in problem-solving activities such as simulations about budget cuts and improved supervision, and in the study of ethical dilemmas. Those learning activities must be organized into a more systematic focus on values development and values education within our preparation programs. Our suggestions here for sharpening that focus included recommendations for teaching specific knowledge and skills related to values.

We have already begun to communicate the core values of the profession in our daily work. What lies ahead is to develop a systematic and intentional way to educate new professionals about those values.

References

Boyer, E. L. *Campus Life: In Search of Community.* Princeton, N.J.: Carnegie Foundation for the Advancement of Teaching, 1990.

Coupland, D. *Generation X: Tales for an Accelerated Culture.* New York: St. Martins Press, 1991.

Dewey, J. *How We Think.* Lexington, Mass.: Heath, 1933.

Dey, E., Astin, A. W., and Korn, W. *The American Freshman: Twenty-Five Year Trends.* Los Angeles: Higher Education Research Institute, University of California, 1991.

Fischer, K. "A Theory of Cognitive Development: The Control and Construction of Hierarchies of Skills." *Psychological Review,* 1980, 87, 477–531.

Kitchener, K. S., and King, P. M. "Reflective Judgment: Concepts of Justification and Their

Relationship to Age and Education." *Journal of Applied Developmental Psychology*, 1981, 2, 89–116.

Kitchener, K. S., and King, P. M. "The Reflective Judgment Model: Transforming Assumptions About Knowing." In J. Mezirow and Associates, *Fostering Critical Reflection in Adulthood: A Guide to Transformative and Emancipatory Learning.* San Francisco: Jossey-Bass, 1990.

Krathwohl, D., Bloom, B., and Masia, B. *Taxonomy of Educational Objectives: The Classification of Educational Goals.* Vol. 2: *Affective Domain.* New York: McMay, 1974.

Meyers, C. *Teaching Students to Think Critically: A Guide for Faculty in All Disciplines.* San Francisco: Jossey-Bass, 1986.

Mezirow, J., and Associates. *Fostering Critical Reflection in Adulthood: A Guide to Transformative and Emancipatory Learning.* San Francisco: Jossey-Bass, 1990.

Perry, W. *Forms of Intellectual and Ethical Development During the College Years.* Troy, Mo.: Holt, Rinehart & Winston, 1970.

Raths, L., Harmin, M., and Simon, S. "Perspectives on the Theory." In J. Goodman (ed.), *Turning Points.* Vol. 1: *New Developments, New Directions in Values Clarification.* Saratoga Springs, N.Y.: Creative Resources Press, 1978.

Wood, S. "Toward Renewed Collegiality: The Challenge of the 1990s." *NASPA Journal*, 1991, 29 (1), 2–9.

Young, R. B., and Elfrink, V. L. "Values Education in Student Affairs Graduate Programs." *Journal of College Student Development*, 1991, 32 (2), 109–115.

LEILA V. MOORE *is director of student program development at The Pennsylvania State University, University Park.*

DEBORAH H. HAMILTON *is conflict management specialist at the Center for Conflict Management, The Pennsylvania State University.*

Effective implementation of the essential values involves five strategies: values transmission, values clarification, analysis of moral issues, commitment, and moral action.

Organizational Imperatives for Implementing the Essential Values

Jon C. Dalton

> A man who wishes to make a profession of goodness in everything must necessarily come to grief among so many who are not good. Therefore it is necessary for a prince, who wishes to maintain himself, to learn how not to be good.
>
> —Machiavelli (1954, p. 84)

There is a long tradition of conventional wisdom that argues that to be effective in leadership roles a man or woman must discount moral value considerations. As Machiavelli notes, having to worry about what is ethically right and wrong can put a leader at a severe disadvantage with the majority of others who are not constrained by such sentiments. According to this conventional wisdom, moral considerations are such risky business and so potentially volatile and disadvantageous that they should be avoided at all costs.

While I suspect that few student affairs leaders would subscribe to Machiavelli's cynical view of the place of morality in leadership, there are, no doubt, many who would agree that the use of ethical considerations and essential values as practical guides to decision making in student affairs administration is indeed risky business. In the complex and demanding leadership roles of higher education, moral value considerations can appear slippery and subjective compared to practical administrative tasks such as accountability, effectiveness, and efficiency. Yet, as Morrill (1980) argues, values are standards of choice that guide decision making. They are often masked, but all choices and decisions are made with reference to certain standards that we call values. An understanding of these fundamental standards or values gives important insight into the ethical character of an individual or an institution. In fact, I believe that a values-centered leadership style is, in the long run, both desirable and effective. In this chapter, I examine some of the reasons for this conviction.

Derek Bok (1982) writes that the greatest challenges of leadership are not to one's intelligence but to one's character. My own leadership experience in student affairs administration has persuaded me that some of the toughest decisions, the most pressing challenges, concern ethical problems and moral considerations. Student affairs is so full of values issues and moral conflict situations that leaders who are unable to handle the complexities of the moral terrain of leadership roles will inevitably be ineffective. Success in managing such situations is, as Bok argues, not so much a matter of intellectual competence as it is of personal integrity and steadfastness to basic standards of ethical practice.

From a practical standpoint, a formal and active advocacy of essential values by student affairs leaders is important for a number of reasons. First, whether or not student affairs professionals choose to identify and articulate a particular core of essential values, they will inevitably communicate values in their decisions, behaviors, and role modeling. This is especially true for student affairs leaders. There is no escaping the communication of values no matter how much one tries to espouse a values-neutral position. All we have to do is inspect our choices and decisions to discover how inescapable values are. Morrill (1980) claims that we invariably find that values form the bedrock of decisions. The central issue for student affairs leaders, therefore, is not *whether* they should advocate certain essential values but *which* values should be advocated and *how* these values can be advocated in a clear and intentional manner.

The case has collectively been made in this volume for a core of eight essential values. These core values form an appropriate canon for student affairs staff since the eight values have had widespread confirmation in both research and professional practice over a long period of time. In the research of Dalton, Barnett, and Healy (1982), chief student affairs leaders identified almost all of the essential values as the most important values that they sought to convey in their own programs, services, and role modeling. Moreover, the eight essential values are broadly confirmed and reflected in the student affairs literature on student development and administrative practice. I believe that the eight essential values provide an important formal ethical guide to decision making in student affairs administration and can serve as valuable standards for the identification and examination of ethical issues in professional practice.

In this chapter, I examine the issue of values and leadership and discuss how student affairs leaders can utilize the essential values to create values-oriented organizations that promote concern for ethical issues and development. I also explore ways in which the essential values can be integrated into the student affairs organization so as to influence policy, programming, and staff development.

Avoiding Indoctrination

Any discussion of essential values must address the issue of indoctrination since this has long been one target of the chief criticisms of values-centered leadership. Unfortunately, student affairs staff too often conclude that any advocacy of values in leadership roles entails moralization or indoctrination.

Rokeach (1968) has noted two characteristics of values that are particularly useful in this discussion of indoctrination. He described some values as *instrumental,* that is, process-oriented values that govern the manner in which one makes decisions or takes actions involving other people. Equality, for example, is an instrumental value that conveys the importance of according others a similar measure of rights and privileges in decisions and actions. Likewise, truthfulness is an important instrumental value that emphasizes faithfulness to objective fact and reality. All of the eight essential values described in the present volume are examples of instrumental values because they provide primary standards for the ways in which student affairs staff make decisions and conduct their professional activities. These instrumental values are so basic to the integrity of professional conduct that violation of any one of them can result in great loss of authority and effectiveness.

Rokeach classifies another type of values as *terminal.* These values represent the ends or results of human desires and aspirations. Happiness, fulfillment, health, wealth, and beauty represent some of these terminal values. Terminal values are highly personal and subjective. They are the stuff of religions, social and political ideologies, and individual dreams and desires. While colleges and universities seek to expose students to the many different visions of ultimate human values, they correctly avoid the direct promulgation of specific terminal values since to do so could constitute deliberate indoctrination.

Rokeach's distinction between instrumental and terminal values is critical since it demonstrates that some values (instrumental ones) can be used as ethical standards without indoctrinating students. The eight essential values described in this volume are instrumental or process values that pertain to *how* individuals manage their professional conduct, especially how they treat other people.

Indoctrination, on the other hand, involves the transmission of specific terminal or ultimate values as the most worthy or real. This distinction is important for student affairs staff since they are rightly concerned about moral indoctrination and may perceive that any talk about values, especially essential ones, somehow entails indoctrination.

It is one thing to advocate that people should be treated fairly, equally, truthfully, justly, and so on; it is quite another matter to prescribe the content of their beliefs, visions, and ultimate convictions. The essential values are instrumental standards for guiding professional practice so that the greatest number of people in the widest range of circumstances will be treated fairly. Moreover, the essential values are so grounded in the core values of higher education that it is difficult to imagine a modern college or university in which there was serious debate about the worth of such essential values as truthfulness, freedom, justice, and community.

The problem with implementing the essential values in student affairs practice is the problem one always encounters when attempting to apply standards to practice. There are several possibilities: (1) to say and not do, (2) to do and not say, (3) to not say and not do, and (4) to say and do. Many people despise the first, admire the second, fear the third, and hope for the fourth. One of the reasons that student affairs staff may be reluctant to discuss values openly is an uncertainty about just what constitutes the essential values of their work. It is difficult to say and do when there is uncertainty about core values. The eight essential values can, therefore, provide an important values baseline for student affairs staff who confront these uncertainties and want a more clearly articulated and relevant set of values for professional practice.

Values-Centered Leadership

Kuh (1983) argues that in high-performance organizations, staff share a core of values or beliefs. Peters and Waterman (1982) observed this same characteristic in their examination of some of America's best-run companies. The evidence suggests that organizations tend to be more productive and efficient when staff members have a clear sense of what they are trying to do and how their efforts are interrelated. This is especially so in education and human services organizations where productivity measures are very difficult to quantify.

The identification of values that are central to the organization can help individuals feel a sense of common purpose and mission. The most effective organizations are those in which leaders articulate and model core values and create organizational structures that integrate the essential values in routine activities and procedures.

One of the ways in which essential values can be given more importance in organizations is by affirming and transmitting them in open and visible ways. Of all the means that help to transmit values to members of the organization, none is as powerful as the behavior and being of the leader. The chief student affairs officer should be an embodiment of the central values of the division. He or she should set the values agenda for the staff.

Some years ago while teaching a leadership class, I invited two colleagues, a vice president for academic affairs and a vice president for development, to speak to the class on a practical leadership problem involving an ethical issue. I asked them both to respond to the same case situation so that the class could analyze any differences and similarities in their responses.

The case situation concerned a public controversy over a faculty member who was having a sexual affair with an older graduate student in one of his classes. The vice president for academic affairs opened his remarks with the declaration, "The first thing I would do is rule out all political considerations." He went on to argue that unless the relationship adversely impacted the faculty member's duties and responsibilities or the student's welfare, the faculty member's personal life was his own business.

The vice president for development opened his presentation by declaring, "The first thing I would do is to consider the political implications of the issue." He went on to argue that the community's interest in and concern about the moral conduct of faculty was of primary importance to him.

The class and I were intrigued and not a little confused about the opposing viewpoints of institutional leaders in addressing this moral situation. Their responses reflected the particular values orientation of each individual. We had witnessed an illustration of how values influence leadership strategies and decisions.

A values-centered leader is one who transmits values both inside and outside the organization. The transmission of values is typically accomplished in the following ways:

Role Modeling. Leaders communicate essential values through personal example. Role modeling is one of the most powerful means of transmitting essential values since it embodies both words and action.

Communicating Values. Organizations take values more seriously when leaders talk about values and engage employees in discussions about values issues. What leaders talk about and spend time communicating reflects the things that they regard as important or valuable. When leaders take the time to focus on values and values issues, they indicate to others that these issues have legitimacy within the organization. They also encourage a broader forum for the discussion of such issues throughout the organization.

Promulgation of Rules, Policies, and Regulations. Leaders transmit values through the rules and procedures that they initiate or endorse in the organization. Such rules and policies define the norms of acceptable conduct and reveal the basic values of the organization.

Personal Advocacy. Leaders transmit values through their personal advocacy of issues, causes, values, and positions. Because of their great public visibility, the advocacy of leaders is often very influential in conveying the values of the organization.

Celebrating Traditions. Another important means of transmitting values, especially in student affairs organizations, is through the celebration of traditions and customs. The celebration of traditions, customs, and special events helps to create social bonds among staff and to promote a sense of shared values. As Roberts (this volume) shows, taking time throughout the year to recognize and celebrate important events and special times helps to promote a feeling of community and to reinforce the other essential values of the organization. In the hectic pace of student affairs work, such events can become especially important because they help staff members renew contacts, share their common problems, and celebrate the accomplishments and challenges of their work.

Implementing the Essential Values: Five Approaches

Effective implementation of the essential values in student affairs practice depends on an understanding of how individuals acquire values and of which strategies are most effective in promoting values. There is not enough space in this chapter for a detailed discussion of all of the methods involved in values acquisition (for more resources, see Moore and Hamilton, this volume; Superka and others, 1976), so I focus here on five strategies that have particular relevance to implementation of the essential values in student affairs organizations.

The five values approaches presented here are distinct leadership strategies for promoting and enhancing essential values in student affairs organizations. There are many such strategies, but these five have special relevance for student affairs staff. These strategies come from my review of the literature on values education as well as from research involving how student affairs leaders approach values issues in their work.

Values Transmission. The values transmission approach involves the direct communication of essential values to employees. Student affairs leaders who use this approach publicly identify the essential values and openly promote them throughout the organization. The transmission approach assumes that the essential values are indeed central to the organization and that there is general agreement about these values. If, as argued throughout this volume, there are certain values that are essential to the profession of student affairs, then it is clear that one of the tasks of the chief student affairs officer is to ensure that the essential values are conveyed to everyone in the organization.

The essential values can be transmitted in a number of ways. They can be referred to in public statements and documents, included in organizational policies and standards, embodied in mission statements and planning priorities, celebrated in traditions, symbols, and other aspects of organizational culture, and simply proclaimed by individuals. I have already indicated that many student affairs leaders express uneasiness about openly conveying values in a way that appears to constitute indoctrination (Dalton, Barnett, and Healy, 1982), yet communication and modeling of values are unavoidable in leadership roles. If certain values are essential to our work, then they must be openly communicated. The transmission approach represents one basic strategy for accomplishing this goal.

Values Clarification. Another strategy focuses on clarifying values issues through reflection and discussion. This approach is often preferred to values transmission since it seems to avoid the overt inculcation of specific values. Student affairs leaders who prefer the clarification strategy generally want to engage their staff in examination of values and values issues in order to encourage introspection, discussion, and peer interaction about essential values.

The values clarification approach can be a very effective means of engaging staff in the examination of current ethical issues and in encouraging their reflection on essential values. Student affairs staff seldom seem to take the time to share their personal values and convictions about the important moral and ethical issues that affect students. Role plays, case studies, and group discussions are examples of values clarification activities that can encourage reflection on the essential values.

Values clarification is often thought to be values-neutral since it does not appear to directly promote specific values. However, it is impossible to avoid the action of transmitting values, no matter how one tries to mask it. Values clarification is an important education strategy for enriching one's understanding of essential values, especially when used in conjunction with values transmission activities.

Analysis of Moral Issues. The research on moral reasoning by Kohlberg (1973), Rest (1973), and Gilligan (1982) clearly demonstrates that individuals reason in different ways about moral problems and that they can be encouraged to develop more sophisticated thinking about moral conflict issues. The implications of this research for student affairs professionals are numerous. For example, student affairs staff need to devote time for discussion and analysis of moral issues in their work with students in order to share perspectives and clarify issues, more sophisticated levels of knowledge and reasoning about values issues can be promoted through efforts to analyze and reason about moral issues, and analysis of moral issues helps staff to recognize that there may be several possible outcomes to values conflicts.

The analysis of moral issues can provide staff with opportunities to share some of their deepest convictions and beliefs about their work with students. At times, such analysis can also be threatening to individuals, since their views about issues may clash with those of others and may touch on highly personal and sensitive matters. It is probably for these reasons that student affairs staff members are often reluctant to engage in structured activities designed specifically for the analysis of values. Such analysis can, however, be a very effective means for both integrating the essential values in student affairs practice and promoting moral reasoning development.

The moral reasoning strategy emphasizes the systematic study of values issues in order to identify specific educational, programmatic, and administrative implications of such issues for professional work and to promote more sophisticated reasoning and understanding of the values issues. The moral reasoning approach is an extension of values clarification but focuses more specifically on rational analysis and less on self-reflection.

Commitment. Whether or not student affairs leaders demonstrate a personal commitment to values is perhaps the single most important factor in encouraging others to take values seriously. It is possible to *talk* about values, to *reason* about them, and to *clarify* them, and yet never to *own* them as one's own. Personal commitment to the essential values is important because others judge the values of leaders by the manner in which they affirm their convictions and beliefs through their actions and decisions.

Nothing is so damaging to ethical leadership as the perception of hypocrisy—that values are simply things to talk about but not demonstrate as acts of personal commitment. Since individuals look to leaders for moral authority, personal commitment is the consistency check, the reliability factor, and the reality test that either affirm or negate the leader's ethical credibility.

Moral Action. One of the most powerful ways to promote the essential values is to provide practical opportunities for individuals to act on the values. Since student affairs endeavors are so full of values issues, it is usually not very difficult to identify ways in which staff can be proactive in acting on the essential values. The use of moral action programs and projects (for example, community service, social action, environmental action, humanitarian aid, and social justice projects) in student affairs organizations can also help staff members to promote shared values and provide very tangible evidence of the commitment of the division to the essential values.

Values Conflicts: They Come with the Territory

From a practical standpoint, some of the compelling issues that confront student affairs leaders today embody intense values conflicts. Issues such as sexual assault, racism, discrimination, academic cheating, alcohol and drug abuse, and multiculturalism compel student affairs professionals to make judgments about values issues and act on them. In earlier times, when there was greater social consensus about core values, it might have been easier to maintain and promote a status quo. Today, however, student affairs staff confront a pluralism of values and life-styles on campus that openly compete and often clash. This situation forces student affairs staff to deal more directly and openly with values issues and to search for a framework of essential values to guide them in the murky world of values conflicts.

Yet, if anything seems certain about the work of student affairs in the twenty-first century, it is that responses to values issues associated with an increasing diversity and pluralism on campus will continue to shape our profession. The essential values described and examined in this volume can provide a valuable framework for student affairs professionals as they struggle to make professional judgments about issues involving values conflicts. Through the integration of the essential values into professional preparation programs and practical in-service training activities, student affairs staff can become better equipped with the awareness and sensitivity needed to deal with contemporary values issues.

In this chapter, I have examined the role of the student affairs leader in transmitting values and using the essential values to build a values-centered organization and leadership style. I have argued that values issues are inescapable in our work and that advocacy of the essential values does not involve moral indoctrination. I have suggested five education strategies that can be utilized by leaders of student affairs organizations to enhance the awareness and utilization of the right values in student affairs practice.

The student affairs profession has struggled throughout its relatively short history with defining its central mission. At different times, it has stressed its primary role as support service, student development, administration, and education. The profession is and probably always will be all of these things, depending on the circumstances confronting student affairs staff. And yet for me and, it would seem, for so many student affairs staff, a central purpose in our work with students is their ethical development as individuals. The opportunity to work with college students in ways that contribute to their development as morally sensitive and responsible individuals seems to be a fundamental reason that so many men and women are drawn to the profession and provides some of its most profound personal gratification. Discussion about the essential values may help to promote more formal attention to the central place of values in student affairs work and to the ethical challenges of our work with college students.

References

Bok, D. *Beyond the Ivory Tower: Social Responsibilities of the Modern University.* Cambridge, Mass.: Harvard University Press, 1982.

Dalton, J. C., Barnett, D., and Healy, M. "Educational Approaches to Values Development in College Students: A Survey of NASPA Chief Student Personnel Administrators." *NASPA Journal,* 1982, *20* (1), 14–21.

Gilligan, C. *In a Different Voice: Psychological Theory and Women's Development.* Cambridge, Mass.: Harvard University Press, 1982.

Kohlberg, L. "Continuities in Childhood and Adult Moral Development Revisited." In P. B. Baltes and K. W. Schaie (eds.), *Life Span Development Psychology: Personality and Socialization.* San Diego: Academic Press, 1973.

Kuh, G. D. (ed.). *Understanding Student Affairs Organizations.* New Directions for Student Services, no. 23. San Francisco: Jossey-Bass, 1983.

Machiavelli, N. *The Prince.* (L. Ricci, trans.) New York: Mentor, 1952.

Morrill, R. *Teaching Values in College.* San Francisco: Jossey-Bass, 1980.

Peters, T., and Waterman, R. *In Search of Excellence: Lessons from America's Best Run Companies.* New York: HarperCollins, 1982.

Rest, J. "Patterns of Preference and Comprehension in Moral Judgment." *Journal of Personality,*
    1973, *41,* 86–109.
Rokeach, M. *Beliefs, Attitudes, and Values: A Theory of Organization and Change.* San Francisco:
    Jossey-Bass, 1968.
Superka, D., and others. *Values Education Sourcebook.* Boulder, Colo.: Social Sciences Educa-
    tional Consortium, 1976.

JON C. DALTON *is vice president of student affairs at Florida State University,
Tallahassee.*

INDEX

Aesthetics, 57–58; and emotion management, 51–52; as essential value, 1, 2, 5, 11–12, 47–48; expression of, 55; and passion and intuition, 56; perception of, 49–51; and student affairs, 56–57; and students as art, 52–55; understanding, 48–49

Altruism, 1, 2, 5, 30–31; and care, 32–33; and human dignity, 7; and humanity, 31; and student affairs, 31–32

American Association of Colleges of Nursing, 49

American College Personnel Association, 61

American Council on Education, 5, 6, 7, 9, 10, 11, 12, 25, 36, 43, 48, 51, 52

Appleton, J., 11

Art, students as, 52–55. *See also* Aesthetics

Arts. *See* Aesthetics

Astin, A. W., 30, 76, 77

Barnet, S., 48, 51, 53, 54
Barnett, D., 88, 92
Barr, M. J., 1
Behavior, and values, 61–63
Bellah, R. N., 20, 27, 31
Ben-David, J., 48
Benet, W., 49
Berdie, R. F., 61
Berger, J., 52
Berman, M., 48
Bloom, A., 26
Bloom, B., 83
Bok, D., 19, 88
Borelli, F., 56, 57
Bowen, H., 16, 17
Boyer, E. L., 17, 29, 30, 31, 32, 37, 81, 83
Briggs, C., 11
Brooks, G. C., 29
Brown, R. D., 32
Browning, D. S., 25
Brubacher, J. S., 30, 47, 48, 50
Burns, E. M., 28
Burton, W., 48

Canon, H. J., 32
Capra, F., 57

Care: and equality, human dignity, and altruism, 25, 32–33; as value, 21–22

Carnegie Commission on Higher Education, 30

Carnegie Foundation for the Advancement of Teaching, 42

Carnegie model, of participatory decision making, 64

Cassirer, E., 49

Chavez, L., 18

Chen, L., 29

Chickering, A. W., 31, 51, 52, 57

Clement, L. M., 2, 22, 25, 34, 80, 82

Clothier, R. C., 5, 6, 7, 8, 11, 61

Coldwell, L. L., 3, 61, 73

Collier, K., 62

Collison, M., 20, 29

Community, 1, 2, 5, 9–11, 35, 44; artifacts of, 39–41; conceptualizations of, 37; definition of, 1, 35–36; and diversity, 42–43; evidence of, 38; and faculty, 41; and involving colleges model, 41–42; and *SPPOV*, 9–10, 11, 35–37, 43–44; and student affairs, 43–44

Cortes, C., 42

Council of Student Personnel Associations (COSPA), 6–7, 9, 10, 55; on community, 10–11; on equality, 9; on human dignity, 6–7

Coupland, D., 77

Cowley, W. H., 1, 2, 5, 6, 8, 9, 10, 53–54

Croce, B., 47, 48, 49–50, 55, 56

Culture, and values, 5

Curriculum, and truth, 16–17

Cyert, R. M., 64

Daft, R. L., 64
Dalton, J. C., 2, 3, 21, 61, 87, 88, 92, 96
De Mebley, G., 28
De Unamuno, M., 51, 55
Decision making: and INVOLVE model, 64–72; participatory, 64; and values, 63–64
Delve, C. I., 32
Dewey, J., 5, 31, 83
Dey, E., 76, 77
Dickinson, E., 50
Dillard, A., 53, 54

ORDERING INFORMATION

NEW DIRECTIONS FOR STUDENT SERVICES is a series of paperback books that offers guidelines and programs for aiding students in their total development—emotional, social, and physical, as well as intellectual. Books in the series are published quarterly in Spring, Summer, Fall, and Winter, and are available for purchase by subscription as well as by single copy.

SUBSCRIPTIONS for 1993 cost $45.00 for individuals (a savings of 20 percent over single-copy prices) and $60.00 for institutions, agencies, and libraries. Please do not send institutional checks for personal subscriptions. Standing orders are accepted.

SINGLE COPIES cost $14.95 when payment accompanies order. (California, New Jersey, New York, and Washington, D.C., residents please include appropriate sales tax.) Billed orders will be charged postage and handling.

DISCOUNTS for quantity orders are available. Please write to the address below for information.

ALL ORDERS must include either the name of an individual or an official purchase order number. Please submit your order as follows:
    Subscriptions: specify series and year subscription is to begin
    Single copies: include individual title code (such as SS1)

MAIL ALL ORDERS TO:
    Jossey-Bass Publishers
    350 Sansome Street
    San Francisco, California 94104

FOR SINGLE-COPY SALES OUTSIDE OF THE UNITED STATES CONTACT:
    Maxwell Macmillan International Publishing Group
    866 Third Avenue
    New York, New York 10022

FOR SUBSCRIPTION SALES OUTSIDE OF THE UNITED STATES CONTACT:
    any international subscription agency or Jossey-Bass directly.